Their Finest Hour

D0851822

by Herbert Lockyer

The Life Beyond
Dark Threads the Weaver Needs
Their Finest Hour
Dying, Death, and Destiny

Their Finest Hour

*Thrilling Moments
in Ancient History*

Herbert Lockyer

Fleming H. Revell
A Division of Baker Book House Co
Grand Rapids, Michigan 49516

Published by Fleming H. Revell
a division of Baker Book House Company
P.O. Box 6287, Grand Rapids, MI 49516-6287

Paperback edition published 1995

Printed in the United States of America

ISBN 0-8007-5589-8

To Leonard and Norah Thurlow, bountiful friends of long standing, whose finest hours are spent in the service of the Master they truly love

Contents

8   Contents

Introduction

ALAS! THE TITLE of this volume in your hands, like Elisha's axe head that fell into the water, is *borrowed*. It is taken from one of the passionate, electrifying speeches of Winston Churchill, in the British Parliament during the dark and ominous days of World War II. German forces seemed to be irresistible in their conquest of Europe, leaving much destruction and death behind them as they ravaged cities and towns in their gory, triumphal advance.

These were, likewise, terrible days for Britain when some of its important centers were almost reduced to rubble through constant, disastrous air raids during the unchallenged superiority of the German Air Force in the early stages of the war. As the war progressed, the stage was reached when the evident possibility of the island being invaded had to be faced and every precaution of defense was taken. It was at this time that Churchill, then prime minister, made his fearless, challenging war speeches. In his rallying call given at the Guildhall, London, November 9, 1939, as the country wiped its wounds through death-dealing air raids, Churchill said: "The maxim of the British people is 'Business as usual.' " When, in 1940, the toll of devastation and death became greater and bitter days were experienced, Churchill addressed the House of Commons on May 13 and gave utterance to the memorable words:

> I would say to the House, as I said to those who have joined this Government, I have nothing to offer but blood, toil, tears, and sweat. We shall not flag nor fail. We shall fight in France, we shall fight on the seas and oceans, we shall fight with growing confidence and growing strength in the air, we shall defend our island, whatever the cost may be. We shall fight on the beaches, we shall fight on landing grounds, we shall fight in the fields and in the streets, we shall fight in the hills; we shall never surrender.

But, when in that year, France fell and it was felt that the brutal German warlords were coming closer to the gates of Britain, Churchill gave Parliament a moving, eloquent speech that stirred the nation to defense—the nation of which he said in his address to Parliament on August 20, 1940:

> Never in the field of human conflict was so much owed by so many to so few.

which speech remains as one of the most appealing utterances of history. Before that he had told the House of Commons:

> Let us therefore brace ourselves to our duties and so

bear ourselves that, if the British Empire and its Commonwealth last for a thousand years men will still say, *"This was their finest hour."*

It was doubtless this glowing tribute to Britain's brave and dauntless stand against Hitler's plundering armies that sprang to my mind as I came yet once again to that arrestive page in sacred history crammed with the brief records of those heroes of faith who reached their finest hour as they endured perils, toil, pain, and martyrdom because of their love of eternal realities. Here is the scroll of blood and tears as given in the New International Version in Hebrews 11:32–40:

> And what more shall I say? I do not have time to tell about Gideon, Barak, Samson, Jephthah, David, Samuel and the prophets, who through faith conquered kingdoms, administered justice, and gained what was promised; who shut the mouths of lions, quenched the fury of the flames, and escaped the edge of the sword; whose weakness was turned to strength; and who became powerful in battle and routed foreign armies. Women received back their dead, raised to life again. Others were tortured and refused to be released, so that they might gain a better resurrection. Some faced jeers and flogging, while still others were chained and put in prison. They were stoned; they were sawed in two; they were put to death by the sword. They went about in sheepskins and goatskins, destitute, persecuted, and mistreated—the world was not worthy of them. They wandered in deserts and mountains, and in caves and holes in the ground. These were all commended for their faith, yet none of them received what had been

promised. God had planned something better for us so
that only together with us would they be made perfect.

In the following chapters I have endeavored to suggest
what I deem to be the finest hours reached by some of the
well-known figures in Scripture as they climbed the steep
ascent to heaven. Other lovers of the Word may feel that
different events are more stirring in the lives of the saints I
have chosen. So be it! Now, at ninety-three years of age,
my finest and most momentous hour came when, as a lad
just over eighteen, the Lord met and saved me with an
everlasting salvation. What an hour that was when, as a
poor youth, I cried for mercy and the Lord heard me, and
has continued with me through my long pilgrimage! My
most sublime hour, however, will come, before very long
now, when I shall see the glorious Face of Him who saved
me by His matchless grace.

1

God and His Fine Hour of Approbation

As THE LORD from everlasting to everlasting, God is Eternal and therefore timeless. His years have no end. In His abode above, what we call *time* is not recognized. There it is one eternal now. God's life and actions are not associated with sections or portions of time we know as years, months, weeks, days, and hours. Time is only related to the successive states of the universe in which we live, move, and have our being, and in which man is a creature of time.

Yet the marvel is that the Timeless One Himself created this universe and in doing so brought into it *time* divided up as days, with each creative day being a period marked off by a beginning and ending. Thus, the first day of Creation was connected with light (Genesis 1:3–5). Originally, then, day meant part of the solar day of twenty-four hours, with its morning and evening (Genesis 1:14–19). In seven days, the heavens and the earth were finished and all the host of them, as well as the creation of the world's first two human beings, and so we read:

> And on the seventh day God ended his work which he
> had made; and he rested on the seventh day from all his
> work which he had made. And God blessed the seventh
> day and sanctified it: because that in it he had rested
> from all his work which God created and made.
>
> Genesis 2:2, 3

Lord Byron gave us the couplet:

> *Time writes no wrinkles on thine azure brow;*
> *Such as creation's dawn beheld, thou rollest now.*

Coming to God's finest hour in His control of the earth He has created, it is not an easy matter to pinpoint a particular period of time, for in His manifold dealings with men in ancient times there were great and glorious hours as, for example, when He triumphed over the pursuing Egyptian hordes at the Red Sea.

But, personally, I feel that God's finest hour was one of approbation as He surveyed His masterpiece of Creation, the record of which is condensed for us in fifteen words oozing with satisfaction over such a wonderful performance. "And God saw every thing that he had made, and, behold, it was very good" (Genesis 1:31). Holy pride of accomplishment filled the Divine heart. God ever rejoices over His works (*see* Psalms 104:31).

God's created world was *good* until man appeared in it, then it became very good, seeing he came in the image of his Creator. Thus, contemplating all that had been created, God saw everything He had made answering to the plan which His eternal wisdom had conceived, and answered, "Behold, it was very good" (Genesis 1:31). But He never pronounced it very good till He had seen it so.

All God's works are still under His eyes, for He ever

reflects upon all wisdom of the products His power provides and is satisfied. Does not this *fine hour* of approbation over a task perfectly accomplished set us an example of reviewing our day's task? May the last hour before entering upon the rest of the night ever be one of inner joy and satisfaction that we have lived and labored for the glory of God.

2

Enoch and Elijah and Their Fine Hours of Translation

AMONG THE MILLIONS who have thronged the earth, all have died with *the exception of only two men*, who never tasted death, but went from earth to heaven in their human bodies. They never saw death, for God translated them to His own immediate presence above in a moment of time. Enoch and Elijah share the unique honor of being the conspicuous two among countless millions who have lived and died, over whom death had no dominion. These two men alone never knew the sting of death. They passed from the temporal into the eternal, with the ease of going from one room to another. And both of these Old Testament prophets had their grand and glorious hours, making it difficult to isolate any hour as their finest. Still, let us look up these ancient saints, separately, and discover if any hour became full and complete for them.

Enoch, the seventh man from Adam, occupies little space in Scripture, some eight verses in all. Yet the little recorded concerning his life and labors is sufficient to make him one of the most fascinating and compelling characters of Holy Writ—certainly the brightest star in the ancient patriarchal age. "The book of the generations of Adam" (Genesis 5) makes dull, monotonous reading with accounts running on for several generations without any variation from *begat, lived,* and *died.*

But at length there comes a dramatic break in the genealogical list, for one is begotten to become different from all others mentioned. Jared was 162 years of age when he had a son he called Enoch, who was to become a very close, earthly companion of God. Outstanding in the brief biography of this early saint was the experience of compelling interest, namely, the commencement of a walk with God after he begat his first child, Methuselah—a walk that continued, without interruption, for 300 years and ended with a blissful conclusion. The first son born to Enoch has the recorded reputation of being the oldest man who ever lived, for Methuselah died at the age of 969.

Becoming a father brought Enoch to the realization of divine Fatherhood, and to a spiritual birth. Hitherto identified with the "wandering stars to whom is reserved the blackness of darkness for ever" (Jude 13), which he came to prophesy against, Enoch was transformed by grace, and forsaking the ungodly, became the godliest of men for the next 300 years. He had walked without God in a profane world, but a reconciliation took place, and the blessed, privileged, and very long fellowship with God commenced. As two cannot walk together except they be agreed (*see* Amos 3:3), the beginning of Enoch's walk with God testifies to the fact that a spiritual agreement between them took place at the birth of Methuselah.

Then there came an unbroken friendship with God that lasted for three centuries, during which long period Enoch had the testimony "that he pleased God" (Hebrews 11:5)—such pleasure arising out of the faith that God is, and that He is the rewarder of them that diligently seek Him. The repeated phrase *walked with God* reveals a real union of hearts. The innumerable hours of holy and happy intercourse which God and Enoch maintained through so many years must have been remarkable; and likewise a constant rebuke to those who walked the way of Cain during the corrupt age necessitating and culminating in the flood.

Walking with God each day brought nearer the divine goal. In unbroken companionship with his heavenly Friend, Enoch found himself gradually weaned from the world, and made ripe for heaven. He did not attempt to walk alone to heaven, but walked *with* God, taking each step with his eyes fixed on his precious Companion. Daily Enoch complied with the will of God, concurred in all His designs, and became a *worker* together with God, as well as a *walker* with Him. He not only walked after God as the saints are exhorted to, but walked *with* Him, as if in heaven already.

This is why the sacred record, instead of saying, "Enoch *lived*," goes on to the double declaration, "Enoch walked with God" (Genesis 5:22). At long last, the glorious moment came when Enoch was not walking with his divine Companion on earth, for his relatives and friends woke up one morning and discovered that "he was not; for God took him" (Genesis 5:24). Enoch became a missing person those nearest to him could not trace. The Epistle to the Hebrews informs us that he was "translated that he should not see death; and was not found" (Hebrews 11:5). In the Genesis narrative we have the monotonous repetition of the phrase concerning all other descendants of Adam—*and he died.* But Enoch did not have such an end—"God took him."

Strange though it may seem, Enoch named his son Methuselah, meaning, *He dies,* and thus, although he came to be the man who lived longest on earth, at length he, too, died. The birth of this son was a never-to-be-forgotten hour in the life of Enoch who lived for 365 years—a year for every day of our normal year. Such a birth, however, was not Enoch's most sublime hour. During his 300-year walk with God there must have been outstanding, glorious days when Enoch had marvelous insights into the divine mind and purpose—days of heaven upon earth. But we feel that Enoch reached *his finest hour* when, one day, while taking his long, accustomed walk with God it seemed as if the two were loathe to part, and so God said to His companion in whom He had pleasure, "Enoch, why go home? Come all the way with Me," and the two went to the Father's home, to continue without a break in their companionship for ever hereafter.

For all the saints of God who strive to walk before and with Him, their finest hour will come when they hear the Bridegroom's voice at His return, saying, "Rise up, my love, my fair one, and come away!"

In the First Book of Kings we read of Elijah. What a compelling contrast these only two raptured, deathless souls in world history present! Enoch's career is compressed into a few verses of Scripture, while Elijah is more widely portrayed, both in the Old and New Testaments, than any other character.

Mystery and majesty are associated with this man of iron, the mightiest of the prophets, austere in manner and dress, and familiar with deserts and solitude. Fearless in his reproof of prevailing evils, conspicuous hours highlight his turbulent career. What a great hour—some readers may think his finest hour—that must have been when, commanded of God to go and stand before King Ahab, Elijah obeyed and declared the terrible famine of three years, which ended in the destruction of the false prophets of Baal.

What further, unforgettable hours there must have been when, tired and hungry, he was fed by an angel! But what a sad hour that was when, overwrought by his tremendous tasks, he asked God to take away his life. God's tender care of the prophet quickly restored his confidence, not only by feeding him, but by giving him a unique display of His miraculous power. What another impressive hour that was when Elijah was sent by God to Ahab to pronounce his doom because of his disobedience and covetousness. The king's final repentance, however, brought him a brief respite from the pronounced judgment.

God was gracious in providing His exhausted prophet with beneficial angelic ministrations. He brought Elisha into the closing period of Elijah's colorful and striking career, and the two became inseparable friends, with Elisha ministering unto Elijah through the days of his prophetic service. When Elijah cast his mantle—symbol of delegated divine power—upon Elisha, it meant the recognition of this son of Shaphat as his successor in office. And so it was that, when the translation of Elijah was to take place, Elisha was there in spite of the occasions when Elijah wanted to go to Bethel, Jericho, and Jordan alone.

What an ever-to-be-remembered hour that was at Jordan, when Elijah smote and divided the waters there, and the two prophets went over on dry ground; and then came Elijah's kind question to his close companion, "Ask what I shall do for thee, before I be taken away from thee." Elisha's answer was no easy one. Knowing that God had anointed Elijah with power, he requested, "I pray thee let a double portion of thy spirit be upon me" (2 Kings 2:9). Elijah answered that if his friend witnessed his translation, that his request would be granted. When Elisha saw

Elijah no more, he quickly exercised the power of Elijah's mantle he was heir to, represented in the course of his ministry when he performed twice as many miracles as Elijah—fulfillment of the double portion Elijah had promised.

At last, it was true of Elijah, as of Enoch, "he was not, God took him." The aspect of the rapture of these two men differed somewhat. Although, as a prophet, Enoch prophesied against the ungodly sinners of his time, as Elijah came to do in his ministry, he does not appear to be as forceful as his copartner in escaping death. There was not the same spectacular appearance. Thus, one day after a long, blessed walk together God lovingly said to Enoch, "Come all the way home with Me today."

But with Elijah the rapture was more dramatic for he went up into heaven by a whirlwind—which was in keeping with the somewhat whirlwind life he had lived. His witness was stirring and revolutionary in nature, and his translation brought him to *his finest hour,* namely, the vision of Him, Elisha spoke of as "the Lord God of Elijah" (2 Kings 2:14). No hour in all his memorable life was comparable to that which brought him into the immediate presence of the God he had so fearlessly and faithfully served. At the rapture of the saints, when, as Enoch prophesied, the Lord will appear with ten thousands of His saints, "a shout, with the voice of the archangel, and with the trump of God" (1 Thessalonians 4:16) will herald the union of saints from heaven and the raptured saints from earth, bringing the true church of God to her finest hour. This is the "one hope" to which she presses, "with every grace endued."

> *Some from earth, for glory some,*
> *Severed only till He come.*
>
> IRA D. SANKEY

3

Abraham and His Fine Hour of Sacrifice

IN HAMLET, Shakespeare has the phrase, "You come most carefully upon your hour" (1.1.5). A thoughtful study of Abraham's life convinces one that this constant companion of God came upon many hours *carefully*, resulting in the patriarch becoming the man of faith he was. A few Bible characters have such an aura about them that they compel attention, and Abraham is one of these, whose original name, Abram and his God-given name, Abraham, occur over 300 times in some 20 books of the Bible, making him one of the most outstanding of Old Testament saints.

Further, Abraham is conspicuous in that he had the coveted honor of being named, "the friend of God," three times in Scripture. All the redeemed saints share the same honor, for Jesus called them, "My friends." It was because of this friendly relationship that God said He could not hide anything from Abraham, whose place in the sacred portrait gallery is quite unique, for it was all of grace. This first Hebrew stands out in the religious history of the world in that God chose him to become the father of a new spiritual race, and the file leader of a mighty host. Thus, his revelation of God forms a most important epoch in the formation of a chosen people.

Born in Ur of the Chaldees, of heathen parents, little is known of Abraham until he was seventy-five years old. Before leaving his home for far-off Canaan, there came his revelation of, and from, God, and he willingly surrendered the seen for the unseen when the call came to surrender certainty for an uncertainty in a promised land. God made him the recipient of three promises: *of a country*, Canaan; *of posterity*, as the stars of heaven; *of a spiritual host*, through whom all the families of the earth would be blessed. What a momentous hour that was then, when Abraham went out not knowing whither he went.

Thereafter, many extraordinary, memorable hours came to this friend of God, as, strong in faith, he waited for the fulfillment of divine promises. Coupled with delay were almost insuperable difficulties, but Abraham maintained his confidence in God and became the father of all them that believe. There were, of course, sad and ignoble hours in the life of this "father of the faithful." His record, like the sun, had its dark spots. We have his conduct toward Hagar—two departures—then his departure from Canaan into Egypt during a period of famine, which was surely not of faith—then the double falsehoods with regard to his wife, Sarah. In *A Midsummer Night's Dream*, Shakespeare says, "To ease the anguish of a torturing hour" (5.1.36). What caused Abraham's torturing hours was the forgiving grace of his heavenly Friend.

Abraham was granted the privilege of instituting a sacrificial order which was symbolical and typical of the whole Mosaic economy to come; and the sorest trial of faith came when God commanded him to offer up his son of promise, Isaac, and Moriah brought Abraham to *his finest hour*—a wonderful hour in that it was a preview of Calvary. The offering up of Isaac was an act of faith, and yet a trial of faith, in that he never questioned the severe divine command.

What God wanted was not Isaac's life, but Abraham's heart and He had that, as his willing obedience to God's demand proves. The only son of promise was bound and placed upon the altar, and the knife raised to slay Isaac, and for such a willing sacrifice Abraham received the testimony that he had pleased God. Isaac did not die, a substitute was found, much to the relief of Abraham, who is the only type in Scripture of God the Father. Abraham so loved his Friend that he surrendered his beloved son, but centuries later at Calvary God gave His only begotten Son to die as the Saviour of the world, and no substitute was provided—*He died!* For our redemption, the knife was not prevented at that grim hour from the Saviour's heart. God gave His much loved Son that we should not die the death our sins deserved. As we shall later see Calvary, too, was the finest hour for Jesus, as Moriah was for Abraham.

4

Jacob and His Fine Hour of Revelation

IN GOD'S PORTRAIT GALLERY, the son of Isaac and Rebekah, Jacob, commands attention because of his likeness to Robert Louis Stevenson's characters Dr. Jekyll and Mr. Hyde, the one person with a double and contradictory existence. In Jacob's case the evil Mr. Hyde was sometimes more evident than the commendable Dr. Jekyll. What a mixture of good and bad this grandson of Abraham was! Inconsistencies characterize this man of guile, yet man of prayer. He was selfish, as seen when his brother Esau came in from the fields faint with hunger, and Jacob bargained over the food Esau so desperately needed. Added to his selfishness was a natural crafty and deceitful mind. As I express it in my volume on *All the Men of the Bible:*

> He violated his conscience when he allowed his mother
> to draw him away from the path of honour and integ-
> rity. He practiced deception upon his blind father with
> the covering of kid skins. Then he told a deliberate lie
> in order to obtain a spiritual blessing. He further
> sinned upon most sacred ground, when he blasphe-

mously used the name of the Lord to further his evil plans.

In one of his essays entitled "Experience," Emerson has the phrase, "To fill the hour—that is happiness." If only Jacob had filled all his hours with beneficial, spiritual experiences, what uninterrupted happiness would have been his. But this sharp trader was paid back in his own coin by the deception of Laban. If only he had lived the whole of his life by faith, as he came to die "by faith" (Hebrews 11:21), what a different story would have been his. Disciplined by God through his afflictions, Jacob received a divine call to the promised land, and was blessed with a son who became the foundation of the great Hebrew race.

When it comes to singling out the most prominent hour in Jacob's sojourn, it is a difficult task. Did it come at the spot he came to call Bethel, when he saw in a dream a ladder set up on earth, with the angels of God, ascending and descending on it, and received such a revelation of God and of His purpose concerning Jacob's seed, that when he awoke, he said, "This is none other but the house of God, and this is the gate of heaven" (Genesis 28:17). It was, indeed, an hour Jacob could not forget, and before leaving the sacred place he set up a pillar and called it, "God's House" (Genesis 28:22); and made the vow of giving God a tenth of all he received from Him. Such was the thrill of that hour, that Jacob returned to Bethel under divine direction, purged his followers of all forms of idolatry, and when cleansed received a renewal of the promise of his seed possessing the land. It was at this solemn hour that his name was changed from Jacob, meaning, the *supplanter*, to Israel, implying, *a prince of, or with God.*

Then there was that memorable hour that left its indelible mark on Jacob's body. Without doubt this, too, was a glorious hour in his life leading him to call the place, Peniel, meaning, *the face of God,* "for I have seen God face to face and my life is preserved" (Genesis 32:30). Surely no man could have a finer hour than that of conflict resulting in having power with God and with men. And yet, our choice of Jacob's finest hour of all came when he journeyed to Egypt for a blessed reunion with the favorite son he had mourned as dead for many years.

On the way he tarried at Beersheba, where, one night, he had a vision of God and heard Him call, "Jacob, Jacob." Instantly, he said, "Here am I" (Genesis 46:2). Then came the wonderful announcement that God Himself would go with the host into Egypt, and that they would meet Joseph, and that He would make of them a great nation. What a joyous hour that must have been as the wagons came that Pharaoh sent to bring Jacob and his seed to the land in which his son had become so famous!

What a heart-moving experience it must have been when, finally, Jacob and his family met Joseph! Are not the chapters heart-moving and incomparable, describing Joseph's revelation of himself to the brothers who had sold him as a slave into Egypt, and the sight of the son who was yet alive; the consequent life Jacob had in Egypt where Joseph was second in command to Pharaoh in the control of the country; and finally, the deathbed scene when Jacob made Joseph promise that he would bury his bones, not in Egypt, but in the burying ground in Canaan?

Yes, Jacob's *finest hour* came when Joseph and he met, wept on each other's neck, and Jacob, now Israel, could say, "Now let me die, since I have seen thy face and thou are yet alive" (Genesis 46:30).

5

Joseph and His Fine Hour of Refusal

BORN THE FIRST CHILD OF RACHEL, as Jacob and she were about to leave the employ of Laban, Joseph, the eleventh son of Jacob, stands out as one of the most prominent men of Scripture, meriting honorable mention as the man who kept his record clean.

The life of this renowned hero, as he went from prison to palace, from rags to riches, never loses its fascination for young and old alike. His actual vicissitudes and virtues read like a fairy tale. His gifts and graces, above all his goodness, brought him much greatness. Specific experiences went into the molding of his conspicuous character. Hours, both sad and satisfying, were faced by Joseph as one who feared God. He believed that behind life the Weaver stood and worked His wondrous plan.

What a torturous hour that must have been when, as a lad, he was sold by his brothers into slavery. Yet Joseph, laboring as a slave of Pharaoh, learned how to be faithful to God in hard places. He came to realize that "prison walls do not a prison make." What a dreamer he was! Yet his dreams came true, and, under God, he became an interpreter of dreams. Godly in life, Joseph acknowledged his dependence upon God for illumination of his own dreams, and those of others, and was thus no mere idle dreamer.

When the hour of sudden prosperity came to him, he was not swollen with pride, but remained unspoiled. When hours of honor followed long hours of humiliation, he was not over-elated. When false accusations and the appearance of guilt, bringing unjust punishment, overtook him, he remained silent, believing that his God would justify him. Magnificently, he knew how to return good for evil. The Lord was ever with Joseph, and it was this noticeable feature that won the confidence of his prison master, who "saw that the Lord was with him, and that the Lord made all that he did to prosper in his hand" (Genesis 39:3). Throughout his entire life he manifested unique wisdom, brotherly love, filial devotion, and, above all, utter submission to God. These are the graces that make Joseph a fitting type of Jesus.

Here, again, is one whose story has an irresistible charm about it, who came up against so many great hours likely to be remembered that opinion differs as to Joseph's *finest hour.* For our part, we select his courageous resistance to strong temptation as a full-blooded young man. He had noticeable physical beauty, which was ever a snare to him, but when enamored Potiphar's wife tried to seduce him, "Lie with me," she pleaded; he fled from her presence. The foiled temptress, by a lie, had the victorious youth imprisoned. God, however, was with His child, and because of his refusal to sin the governor showed him mercy in his prison life and gave him favor in the sight of the keeper (*see* Genesis 39:7–23).

6

Moses and His
Fine Hour of Commission

As the only man in the Bible to have had the Almighty God as his undertaker, for we read that, "God buried him" (see Deuteronomy 34:6), Moses must have been an unusual man to merit such a singular honor. This gigantic figure casts his lengthy shadow over Scripture, in which his name occurs over 750 times in some 30 books. His name, meaning, draw out, was given him by Pharaoh's daughter, who ordered him to be drawn out of the water, in which his mother had placed him in a cradle made of bulrushes, in order to escape the cruel edict of the king of Egypt, namely, the death of every male Hebrew child born in the land. Providence is seen in this rescue, for Moses was adopted by Pharaoh's daughter as her son so that he became skilled in the wisdom of Egypt, the land of bondage from which he was to deliver his fellow Hebrews.

Moses lived for 120 years, a period divided into three sections of forty years each. The first forty years, from his birth until the flight into Midian because of his patriotic desire to help his brethren, he learned as Pharaoh's daughter's son to be SOMEBODY. The second forty years, stretching from his flight to the Exodus, with all its varied experiences, he learned how to become a *NOBODY*. The third forty years found him back in Egypt at the repeated command of God, and it was during this period that, as the leader of God's hosts, Moses came to learn that *GOD WAS EVERYBODY*—the God he himself would speak to face-to-face as a friend.

We cannot read the record of Moses, so divinely guided in his life and service, without feeling something of the holy intimacy existing between God and the prophet God looked upon as His *friend*. When he died in the plains of Moab, "his eye was not dim, nor his natural force abated" (Deuteronomy 34:7). Thomas Gray, poet of the eighteenth century, in his "Hymn to Adversity," identifies one as bearing "iron scourge and tort'ring hour." Moses certainly knew of the "iron scourge" and had quite a few "tort'ring hours." Yet not all his hours were of this hard nature. He had his great and noble hours.

Selecting, however, the finest hour of this conspicuous companion of God, is no light task. Doubtless many would say it came when, because of the pursuing Egyptians seeking to slay the Hebrews, they were forced to face the Red Sea, in which, to all appearances, the whole host would be drowned. But fearless, faithful Moses knew that God made the sea; it was His, and He could do as He liked with it. The dramatic hour came when Moses stretched his hand over the sea, and the Lord caused the waters to be divided, providing a safe, dry passage for His people.

Reaching the farther side of the sea, Moses again stretched his hand over the waters, and as they rolled back, the pursuing Egyptians were caught in the middle, and the whole host of them were drowned. Thus, Moses and the children of Israel sang the song of redemption that came to them in the hour the Lord triumphed gloriously over the enemies of His people. Others, when asked to state their opinion regarding Moses' finest hour, may decide that it came when he received the Law on the Mount and, without doubt, this was a sublime hour for him.

The personal choice of many, of the finest hour that came to the lawgiver, was experienced during those lonely days in the backside of the desert, after his flight from Egypt. While caring for the cattle of his father-in-law, Jethro—a lowly task for a man of Moses' wisdom and stature—there came the sublime hour of revelation, of which the rest of the life of Moses was but the unfolding, for it was at this juncture that he received His commission to deliver Israel out of Egypt (Exodus 3).

First there was the marvelous way God was pleased to manifest His glory to Moses. It was in the burning bush, that did not consume, with no fire from earth or heaven kindling it, as far as the temporary shepherd could see. Yet he was to see and know more of God in this desert spot with its extraordinary sight than he had ever had in Pharaoh's court. At first, Moses was afraid of such a sight, but fear vanished when he came to perceive that God was in the bush that burned but was not consumed. It was here at Horeb that he received the declaration of God's grace and goodwill to His people, whom He loved for their father's sake. It was here, too, that Moses learned of God's purpose concerning the deliverance of Israel out of Egypt. The narrative records these aspects of the call of Moses as the deliverer of the people:

God's purpose, as to the exodus was explicit—it was imminent, for He was coming down to deliver.
God gave Moses the commission to act in this deliver-

ance as His ambassador, both to Pharaoh and to Israel, and full instructions as to what to say to both.

God answered the objection of Moses regarding his unworthiness for such a task, assuring him of His constant presence and protection.

God, in His goodness, assured His servant beforehand what the triumphant issue would be.

Surely, no hour in the life of Moses could surpass this remarkable hour at the burning bush—*the finest hour* in the career of this faithful servant of God! It was here that God spoke of His knowledge of the sorrows of His people, and of His desire to give them the oil of joy for mourning. For ourselves, the application of the bush aflame, but not consumed is summed up in the expressive lines of Elizabeth Barrett Browning in her poem "Aurora Leigh":

> *Earth's crammed with heaven,*
> *And every common bush afire with God;*
> *But only he who sees, takes off his shoes,*
> *The rest sit round it and pluck blackberries,*
> *And daub their natural faces unaware*
> *More and more from the first similitude.*

7

Joshua and His Fine Hour of Subordination

JOSHUA HAS BEEN NAMED the first soldier consecrated by sacred history, and what a gallant soldier he was! In his initial call he was exhorted by God, four times over, to be brave and courageous, as he fought the Lord's battles—a quality he continuously manifested right up until he died at the age of 110.

Born in bondage, when his nation suffered in Egypt under Pharaoh, Joshua knew all about the lash of the whip, the almost impossible task of making bricks out of straw, and the deep, national sigh for liberty. Little did he realize, when a slave, that he would become his nation's supreme commander and leader. This is why, when he came to power, his solemn commands were colored by hard experiences of the past.

Joshua was a good soldier of the Lord, and a magnanimous, unselfish statesman. He was preeminent as a military leader who, with imparted wisdom from God, knew how to plan campaigns, discipline his forces, use spies, and emerge victorious because of his allegiance to God and his call to fight His battles. Many a general has closely studied Joshua's strategy and conquest of Canaan.

What a soldier-saint he was who knew how to "trust in God . . . and keep [his] powder dry!" In all his magnificent victories he never stooped to pilfering and plunder. His saintliness came as the result of being filled with God, enjoying the presence of God, indwelt by the Word of God, and obedient to the will of God (Deuteronomy 34:9; Joshua 1: 5, 8; 5:14; 6:27; Numbers 32:12).

Many striking hours can be identified in the victorious career of Israel's premier: such as the parting of the waters of Jordan providing Israel a dry passage to Canaan; the conquest of Jericho, of Ai, of the kings of the Amorites; and then the masterful task of settling the tribes in the promised land with Israel serving the Lord. These are wonderful episodes and one of them, at least, deserves to have the honor of being the most glorious hour in the onward march of Joshua. But in our reckoning, the most imposing hour came to him at Jericho where he had an encounter with a man facing him with a drawn sword in his hand.

Challenging him, Joshua asked, "Art thou for us, or for our adversaries?" Then came the astonishing reply, "Nay; but as captain of the host of the Lord am I now come." That the personage was not an angel is evidenced by the fact that immediately Joshua fell on his face to the earth and worshiped saying, "What saith my Lord unto his servant?" (Joshua 5:13, 14).

A further indication that this *Captain* was not a human, but a divine being is seen in his fiat: " 'Loose thy shoe from off thy foot; for the place whereon thou standest is holy.' And Joshua did so" (v. 15). The presence of the *Captain* made it holy ground. A few verses down we read of those who "passed on before the Lord." Joshua had been in command of the forces of Israel. God had commissioned him to command people and priests alike (Joshua

3:3–8; 11:15)—and a most efficient commander he proved
to be. But now another appears on the scene to captain the
host of the Lord, and Joshua did not seem to be ruffled by
His appearance and purpose. Why? No fault could be
found in Joshua's leadership up to this point. Matthew
Henry comments that "Joshua was at his post as a general,
when God came and made Himself known as Generalis-
simo." For the tremendous tasks ahead Joshua needed
God at his side to help him act valiantly, and the drawn
sword in the hand of the Captain assured him that God
was ready to defend His people.

As Jesus is referred to as a "leader and commander to
the people"; and as the "captain of our salvation" (Isaiah
55:4; Hebrews 2:10), we have no hesitation in thinking
that the soldierlike person Joshua saw was the Son of God
in one of His preincarnation appearances, and who fre-
quently appeared in human form, and who here takes
over as Commander-in-Chief, as Captain, both of Joshua,
and the host of Israel, and also of the host of angels to
assist in coming triumphs. As for Joshua, he had *his finest
hour* when he subordinated to the heavenly Captain, and,
willing to take orders from another, asked, "What saith
my Lord, unto his servant?" (Joshua 5:14).

The greatness of Joshua's soldierlike spirit is seen when
he fell to the earth and worshiped Him who had come to
assume overall leadership of Israel. Above all other men,
Joshua knew how to command, and consequently knew
how to obey, and with his Captain went forth conquering
and to conquer. For ourselves, as we endeavor to fight the
good fight of faith, our finest hour will come when we
discover that it is only the Captain of our salvation who is
able to strengthen us, so that we, too, can be victorious
and be made "perfect through our sufferings" in His service.

8

Samson and His Fine Hour of Vengeance

As Samson is named among the heroes of faith in the Bible's Hall of Fame as one who, by faith, "obtained promises, stopped the mouth of lions," and who, "obtained a good report through faith" (Hebrews 11:32, 33, 39), we feel that he should have a niche in our gallery of those who experienced a finest hour in life. The son of the Danite, Manoah, Samson became the most spectacular of the Hebrew judges, and judged Israel for twenty years. He is also among the few in Scripture whose birth and manner of life were foretold. Angelic visitation to Manoah and his barren wife, with divine assurances that the son born to them would be a deliverer of Israel from bondage to the Philistines for forty years, led them to confess that they had seen God.

Born and brought up a Nazarite, Samson was unconquerable so long as his vow was unbroken, but his self-indulgence after revealing the secret of his Nazarite strength to the seducing Delilah, brought shame and degradation to him who always acted single-handed and alone in his exploits. He asked for no assistance, never called the armies of Israel together in his conflict with the Philistines, but without human aid acted in his own unconquerable strength. The curtain is drawn over how he managed his court as judge, over the wisdom of his judgments, and over the manner of Israel's life for a whole generation under her gigantic ruler.

Separated unto God from his birth, mixed or foreign marriages and laxity of sexual relationship brought Samson, with all his prowess, to many dark and drudging hours. He has been referred to as an example "of impotence of mind in body strong." C. W. Emmet, in his study on *Samson*, says that "the conspicuous Judge teaches us that bodily endowments, no less than spiritual, are a gift from God, however different may be the modern conception of the way in which they are bestowed, and that their retention depends on obedience to His laws." Mighty in physical strength, Samson was yet weak in resisting temptation.

The secret of his incomparable physical and muscular strength comes out in the thrice-repeated phrase, "The Spirit of the Lord came mightily upon him" (Judges 13:25; 14:6, 19). But after he had betrayed his Nazarite secret, and fell asleep on the lap of Delilah, the Philistines cut off his long locks of hair, visible token of his divine unction, "and his strength went from him," and when he awoke, "he wist not that the Lord was departed from him" (Judges 16:19, 20). Then came the goring out of his eyes, and the constant grinding in the prison house. "Eyeless in Gaza, at the mill with slaves," as John Milton expressed it. Forgiving grace, however, can be seen in that the hair of his head, visible sign of his former Nazarite power, began to grow again. This encouraged Samson to beseech God to divinely strengthen him, only once more, that he might exercise a final and fatal judgment upon the Philistines, with whom he was prepared to die.

This now blind and battered judge of Israel had had impressive hours of victory over the nation's foes. What an elated hour that was when he tore in pieces, with nothing in his hand, the young lion that roared against him! But when he caught 300 foxes and ingeniously used them to burn up the cornfields and vineyards of the Philistines, it only ended in the disastrous burning of the wife of Samson, who had been taken from him, and her father. But this led to the great hour when Samson avenged such a crime by smiting the Philistines hip and thigh, with a great slaughter. Soon after, the Spirit of the Lord came mightily upon him again, and with a jawbone of an ass he slew 1000 men.

But Samson's finest hour, although it was to be his final hour on earth, came when the Philistines gathered together to offer sacrifice unto Dagon their god, for delivering Samson into their hands. This was to be their time of rejoicing over Israel's formidable judge. So he was brought from the prison house to the house of Dagon to be made a laughing stock of by 3000 men and women, including all the lords of the Philistines. Samson, however, besought the Lord God to endow him with unusual strength yet once more that he might take vengeance upon his enemies for blinding and battering him in his helpless condition.

It may be questioned whether it is right to associate vengeance with a fine hour as we have. What must not be forgotten is the distinction between vengeance and revenge. Revenge can be hard and cruel and vindictive, meting out a retaliation far beyond the desert of the offense committed. Vengeance is a divine quality, and therefore never unjust. "Vengeance is mine, I will repay, saith the Lord" (Romans 12:19). "The Lord hath taken vengeance for thee of thine enemies" (Judges 11:36). The Greek word for vengeance, literally, means *that which proceeds out of justice*, and not, as with human revenge, out of a feeling of indignation. All the judgments of God are holy and right, and free from any element of spite, self-gratification, or vindictiveness. It was in this way that God enabled Samson to avenge himself of his enemies.

That God answered Samson's prayer for a last endowment of power is evident in what happened when a lad placed him between the two middle pillars supporting the roof of the massive temple of Dagon, and with his hand on the right pillar, and the other hand on the left pillar, Samson bowed himself with all his God-given might, and the house fell, and 3000 men and women who came to make sport of Samson, were slaughtered by him. "So the dead which he slew at his death were more than they which he slew in his life" (Judges 16:30). Truly, this was *his finest hour!*

In Milton's "Samson Agonistes," the poet presents Samson as an example of patriotism and heroism in death, to all who "from his memory inflame their breast to matchless valour and adventures high." Into his hands God placed "invincible might" to quell the oppressor, and Gaza mourned over this "faithful champion" who "bore witness gloriously."

> *Samson hath quit himself*
> *Like Samson, and heroically hath finish'd*
> *A life heroic.*

9

Ruth and Her Fine Hour of Decision

No BIBLE LOVER ever tires of reading the entrancing story of Ruth, made up of only eighty-five verses, and wedged in between Judges and 1 Samuel. Benjamin Franklin, the American statesman and philosopher, ridiculed at one time in Paris for his defense of the Bible, was determined to find out how much of it his scoffers had read. He informed one of the learned societies that he had come across a story of pastoral life in ancient times that seemed to him very beautiful, but he would like the opinion of its members. A night was arranged for Franklin to read to the assembly of scholars a lyric which impressed him. The Bible lover read the Book of Ruth, and when he had finished the scholars were in ecstasies and begged Franklin to print it. "It is already in print," said Franklin. "It is a part of the Bible you ridicule."

How grateful we are that Ruth is in the Bible, in fact, the rest of the Bible from her time could not have been written had the young widow not decided to leave Moab for Bethlehem! From a literary point of view, there is nothing in the entire range of biography, sacred or profane, comparable to the idyllic simplicity, tenderness, and beauty of the love story, which has enchanted succeeding ages, and can be read by all with both pleasure and profit. The Book of Ruth reveals how industrial and labor problems can be solved. Boaz, who became Ruth's husband, was a wealthy farmer, yet maintained a delightful relationship to those who worked in his fields. Meeting his employees, he would say, "The Lord be with thee," and such was the harmony between employer and employees that they would immediately reply, "The Lord bless thee."

The story opens with a Hebrew known as Elimelech, his wife Naomi, and their two sons, Mahlon and Chilion, leaving Bethlehem for Moab because of prevailing famine in the land. Before long, disaster struck their Jewish home in a foreign land when Elimelech died. Naomi's two sons married women of Moab, Orpah and Ruth. Ten years later these sons died.

Grief-stricken and perhaps bitter over those three graves in Moab, Naomi found comfort in her two daughters-in-law, and learning of how the Lord had visited Bethlehem by giving the people bread, she made up her mind to return home. Ruth and Orpah, left without material support because of the death of their husbands, left with Naomi, and all three "went on the way to return unto the land of Judah" (Ruth 1:7). The journey, however, came to a halt, for Naomi knew what it would mean for the two young widows—and Moabites—to go all the way to Bethlehem and face uncertainty in a strange land. So she pled with them to return home, and remarry.

At first, both Orpah and Ruth turned a deaf ear to Naomi's request saying, "Surely we will return with thee unto thy people" (Ruth 1:10). But when Naomi declared that the hand of the Lord had gone out against her, and that because of her age, she was too old to have another husband and other sons, the two young women wept, and Orpah, kissing her mother-in-law took her advice, and went back to her people, and to her gods. Ruth and Naomi watched the retreating form of Orpah, and Ruth uttered her remarkable decision to go with Naomi to Bethlehem in spite of the latter's three-time exhortation to return to Moab.

What a moment that must have been when, with her arms around Naomi, Ruth pleaded:

> Intreat me not to leave thee, or to return from following after thee: for whither thou goest, I will go; and where thou lodgest, I will lodge; thy people shall be my people, and thy God my God:
> Where thou diest, will I die, and there will I be buried: the Lord do so to me, and more also, if ought but death part thee and me.
>
> Ruth 1:16, 17

There can be no question but that this was Ruth's *finest hour*, and history and literature can provide no more exquisite expression of love and loyalty found in this lovely idyll bearing the name of the lover herself. Such beauty of heart, generosity of soul, firm sense of duty and meekness, have placed the winsome portrait of Ruth among the immortals.

That finest hour of decision also brought rich rewards to Ruth, for she became the wife of godly, wealthy Boaz, the mother of Obed, the grandmother of Jesse, and the great grandmother of King David, and the ancestress of the

Lord Jesus, and thus found honorable mention in His genealogy (Matthew 1:5). We praise God for Ruth and her fine hour of choice, for it was from Boaz, an Israelite without guile, and from Ruth, who, as Carl McIntire expresses it, became an "Israelite not in race, but in mind, not in blood but faith, not by tribe, but by virtue and goodness" that Jesus came as the most perfect expression of all the graces we find in the charming Book of Ruth.

10

Samuel and His Fine Hour of Response

THE LAST OF THE ROLE of judges in Israel, Samuel has a place all his own in Jewish history because of his mission in connection with the transition of the nation from a theocracy, in which the people were directly governed by God, to a monarchy, in which they were ruled over by earthly kings. The opening chapters of 1 Samuel present a sad picture of the rivalry polygamy produced. Elkanah had two wives, and, consequently, the family was a divided one, with a division that carried both guilt and grief.

Peninnah was the name of one wife, and Hannah the name of the other woman. The first had sons and daughters by Elkanah, but Hannah was childless—an affliction aggravated by her rival's insolence. Yet her husband seemed to have had a preference for her, and was certainly kind to her as she longed for children by him, assuring her that she meant more to him than ten sons. In bitterness of soul, however, she went to the temple and prayed and wept before the Lord, and made a vow that if God gave her a son, she would give him back to God all the days of his life. Eli was the ministering priest, and noticing Hannah in the posture of prayer, moving her lips but uttering no words censured her for being drunk. Quickly, Hannah protested that she had not taken wine but was pouring out her soul unto the Lord. Then when Eli heard her complaint, he encouraged her, assuring her that God would answer her prayer. Hannah rose, and left the temple, and "her countenance was no more sad" (1 Samuel 1:18).

Shortly after returning home, the miracle happened, for "the Lord remembered Hannah" (1 Samuel 1:19), and she conceived and bore Elkanah a son, and called his name Samuel because "I have asked him of the Lord" (1 Samuel 1:20). As soon as Samuel was weaned, Hannah brought him to Eli and declared her decision to lend her son to the Lord as long as he lived, and Samuel was exclusively the Lord's until death ended his dedication. What a wonderful prophetic prayer that was that Hannah offered, as she surrendered her longed-for son to the Lord! (1 Samuel 2: 1–10).

Under the care and tuition of Eli the priest, Samuel developed, and, on Eli's death, succeeded him in office and exercised the priestly function of intercession, offering sacrifices, pronouncing benedictions, and anointing kings. As a prophet of the Lord, Samuel was faithful, and it was under his courageous pronouncements that Israel renounced her idolatry and shook off the yoke of oppressors.

As the last of the judges, Samuel went round his circuit giving divine judgments upon spiritual and moral questions, and maintaining the hearts of the people, love for the Lord and His Law. In these ways "he judged Israel all the days of his life." When he appointed his sons to succeed him as judges, Samuel was guilty of a parental mistake, for it was this action that gave the people reason for demanding a king, since his sons were so wicked (1 Samuel 8:1–6). But when Samuel died, all Israel lamented him as one of the great heroes of Hebrew history who "through faith . . . obtained promises" (Hebrews 11:32, 33).

As with all other characters we are considering, we are eager to discover the finest hour in this son of Hannah, who became a prophet of the Lord. It is evident from his history that many sublime hours were his as when the Ark of the Lord was recovered from the Philistines and revival broke out at Mizpeh; when the prophet offered a burnt offering unto the Lord for victories at Ebenezer; when he rehearsed all the words of the people regarding their desire for a king, in the ears of the Lord; when he anointed Saul as first king over Israel, and then later anointed David; when he proclaimed the establishment of the kingdom, and also when he called for thunder and rain to destroy the wheat crop because of the wickedness of the people in rejecting the Lord as their reigning Sovereign.

But somehow, the conviction is ours that Samuel's *finest hour* came to him when, as a lad, he served God and Eli in the temple in which he "grew on and was in favour, both with the Lord, and also with men" (1 Samuel 2:26). It was then that the holy intimacy between the Lord and His prophet began, which became an impressive feature throughout Samuel's life. Early in his temple sojourn, Samuel had an unforgettable experience. After Eli and he had retired for the night, the Lord called young Samuel three times, by name, and each time thinking it was Eli who spoke, Samuel responded immediately, "Here am

I"—a good example of instant readiness of the younger to serve the elder. Ignorant that the Lord was calling him, Samuel mistook God's voice for Eli's, for "Samuel did not yet know the Lord" (1 Samuel 3:7). After the third call Eli perceived that it was the Lord who was calling Samuel and gave his young companion instructions as to what to say if the voice called him again. He was to answer, "Speak, Lord, for thy servant heareth" (1 Samuel 3:9).

Shortly after retiring one night, the Lord came and stood by Samuel's bed, and doubling his name this time said, "Samuel, Samuel," and without rising and running as he had before, he lay still, and at once responded, "Speak for thy servant [not Eli's servant, but the Lord's] heareth." Then the Lord went on to confide to Samuel the sad message about Eli's house, and the punishment that would come upon it. When morning came Eli desired to know from Samuel what the Lord had spoken to him about, and he told him all, hiding nothing from his aged master. From this point on Samuel developed, and "the Lord was with him, and did let none of his words fall to the ground," and all Israel came to know that he was "established to be a prophet of the Lord" (1 Samuel 3:19, 20).

The intimate relation between the Lord and His prophet often appears. The Lord revealed Himself to Samuel in Shiloh by the Word of the Lord. When the people came to the prophet, and said, "Give us a king," he went at once and rehearsed the words in "the ears of the Lord" (1 Samuel 8:21). Then when it came to the choosing and anointing of Saul as Israel's first king, a delightful evidence of the confidence God had in His servant, "The Lord had told Samuel in his ear a day before

Saul came," all His purpose concerning him (1 Samuel 9:15).

The Hebrew phrase for "in his ear" reads "He uncovered the ear of Samuel." As a Nazarite, long hair would cover the ears, and as the Lord wanted to convey by a secret whisper to Samuel, His plan, He gently lifted the hair from Samuel's ear so that he could distinctly hear the still small voice. This beautiful touch is described and applied to every child of God in James D. Burns's moving hymn from Ira D. Sankey's *1200 Collection*.

> *O, give me Samuel's ear—*
> *The open ear, O Lord!*
> *Alive and quick to hear*
> *Each whisper of thy word:*
> *Like him to answer at thy call,*
> *And to obey thee first of all!*

The history of Samuel marks him out as an intercessor. Born in answer to prayer and with a name constantly reminding him of the privilege and power of prayer, Samuel ever sought to maintain holy intimacy with God. Listen to phrases like "The children of Israel said to Samuel, 'Cease not to cry unto the Lord our God for us' "; "Samuel prayed unto the Lord"; "Samuel called unto the Lord"; "God forbid that I should sin against the Lord in ceasing to pray for us"; "Samuel cried unto the Lord all night." Do they not reveal a correspondence fixed with heaven? This virtue, and others arising from it, are implied in further verses of Burns's hymn, "Hushed Was the Evening Hymn":

> *O, give me Samuel's heart:*
> *A lowly heart, that waits*

Where in thy house thou art;
    Or watches at thy gates
By day and night, a heart that still
Moves at the breathing of thy will!

O, give me Samuel's mind,
    A sweet, unmurmuring faith,
Obedient and resigned
    To Thee in life and death:
That I may read, with childlike eyes,
Truths that are hidden from the wise!

11

David and His
Fine Hour of Challenge

THE SENTIMENT has been expressed that a biography of any person should be read with an endeavor to find out what were their vital forces, and what were the leading principles that ruled and toned their conduct and relations. Find the one thing that most impresses you in every life, and that will suggest the message God meant to send by making, endowing, and guiding such a person. In the vignettes of biblical characters found in the volume in your hands, this has been the principle guiding us in the selection of the finest hours of their lives, believing that such an hour gave tenor to their character and conduct.

David, the son of Jesse, whose name occurs well over 1,000 times in Scripture, and who began to reign at 30 years of age and reigned for 40 years, was every inch a king. In spite of his sins and failures, which he bitterly lamented, few of the historical figures of the world have been formed in a bigger mold, as J. G. Greenbough suggests, than David who "stands out in huge bulk as one of the world's master minds."

His name, meaning, *beloved,* given by godly parents

who prayed for his coming, and loved him dearly after his birth, became descriptive of his own loving, winsome attractiveness, and endearing personality, so much so that God could speak of David as a man after His own heart. Although anointed to office by Samuel, this second and greatest of Israel's kings is specifically referred to as "The Lord's Anointed" (2 Samuel 19:21; 23:1).

Endowed with a prophetic gift, David was one of those holy men of old, moved by the Holy Spirit to set forth many glorious truths relating to Christ as Saviour and Messiah. He became the greatest personal type of Christ, and had his name adopted by Christ (Isaiah 55:3; Hosea 3:5). In the New Testament David's Psalms are quoted from more often than any other part of the Old Testament. No poetic genius has been more often constantly used and quoted from than this sweet psalmist of Israel, whose Psalms remain as a masterpiece of spiritual literature. In Greenbough's words, David will ever abide as "the inspired poet of the religious affections."

Space forbids us lingering over all that we would like to say in regard to the renowned king of Israel, whose distinguishing peculiarity was the recognition in the most loyal manner of a higher loyalty to God. Tennyson says of David, that he "regarded himself as a mere human vice-regent." Not only was he unique as a poet, and valiant as a warrior—his life had a decided Godward bent.

His defiance and defeat of the mighty Goliath never loses its fascination for the young, and its appeal to the saints never to fear evil forces arranged against them, no matter how formidable, if their trust and confidence are in Almighty Lord God. David had had no training as a fighter, but knew only the care of his father's sheep. Of low estate, and dressed as any other poor country shepherd of his time, Scripture says that "he was ruddy, and withal of a beautiful countenance, and goodly to look to" (1 Samuel 16:12), and Samuel was instructed by the Lord to anoint this handsome, strong, and godly youth as Saul's successor as king. The Spirit of the Lord came upon him at that hour, and in a unique way he was brought into the presence of Saul who was still king, although the Spirit of the Lord had departed from him.

Possessed by an evil spirit Saul became morbid and depressed, and his servants urged him to seek out a skillful player on a harp, whose music would counteract the influence of the evil spirit. One of the servants gave a glowing account of a son of Jesse who would be the very person, and thus Saul sent word to Jesse to send him David, his son, and as soon as the two met, David found favor in Saul's sight, and was made the king's armor-bearer, in addition to being the musician able to calm the agitated mind of Saul when possessed by an evil spirit.

The day came when the massive giant, Goliath, the champion of the Philistines, almost seven feet in height, defied Israel, and challenged their armies to fight him. Battle lines were drawn, and the three elder sons of Jesse followed Saul to the conflict. Young David was back home feeding his father's sheep, and one day was sent by his father to carry food to the three sons, now in Saul's army, and we all know the daring and victorious outcome of David's visit to the camp. It brought him to his finest hour.

David presented himself to Saul, and assured him that as he had slain a lion and a bear attacking his father's sheep, he had no fear of challenging the giant Goliath. Ultimately, Saul commissioned David to fight the Philistine champion, and clothed him with armor for the action.

But the youth discarded the armor, and out he went, no breastplate, no sword, nothing but his rough shepherd clothing, and a sling with five smooth stones taken from a brook.

When the two challengers met, Goliath cursed David by his gods, and threatened to give David's flesh as a tender and delicate meal for the birds. "Am I a dog, that thou comest to me with staves?" (1 Samuel 17:43). But David had more than his sling and pebbles, as his courageous, magnificent challenge indicates when, in all humility, he declared that he had come to deliver Israel on the authority of God, and, therefore, had no doubt as to the victorious issue. There is no challenge in the whole of historical literature comparable to that Goliath received in the words:

> Thou comest to me with a sword, and with a spear, and with a shield; but I come to thee in the name of the Lord of hosts, the God of the armies of Israel, whom thou hast defied. This day will the Lord deliver thee into mine hand; and I will smite thee, and take thine head from thee; and I will give the carcases of the host of Philistines this day unto the fowls of the air, and to the wild beasts of the earth; that all the earth may know that there is a God in Israel. And all this assembly shall know that the Lord saveth not with sword and spear; for the battle is the Lord's, and he will give you into our hands.
>
> 1 Samuel 17:45–47

As the two met, David took only one stone from his bag which, because of his clever and accurate markmanship with a sling, was sufficient, and the stone entered a vulnerable, uncovered part of the giant's forehead, and down he fell face downward. David raced forward, took Goliath's sword, cut off his head, and, at such a gory sight the Philistines fled. Matthew Henry comments that, "David addresses himself to this combat rather as a priest that was going to offer a sacrifice to the justice of God than a soldier that was going to engage an enemy of his country." Yes, David, this was *your finest hour*, because it brought you ultimately to be the king of Israel, and your triumphant challenge became typical of the glorious victories of your Greater Son, Jesus, who made a show of evil forces openly, and who made it possible for us to be more than conquerors over Satan and all the powers of darkness.

12

Solomon and His Fine Hour of Humility

IN TWELFTH NIGHT, Shakespeare has the impressive sentence, "Be not afraid of greatness: some men are born great, some achieve greatness, and some have greatness thrust upon them" (2.5.159). But without humility, greatness is a hollow honor. We need never be afraid of greatness if only it is matched by goodness of character. Solomon was born great, achieved greatness—much of it thrust upon him—but he failed miserably in spiritual and moral goodness. He made a shipwreck of his life, and forever remains one of the most disappointing figures in Hebrew history.

Solomon's life was full of tremendous promise and was blessed with unusual advantages. His parents gave him his name, which means, *The Lord loved him.* In a Psalm for Solomon, he is referred to as the king, and as a king's son (Psalms 72:1). This second child of David, by Bathsheba, received more royal majesty than any king before or after him ever received (1 Chronicles 29:20–25), and became one of the most compelling and illustrious figures in Old Testament history. Eminently gifted by God with great wisdom, Solomon materially developed the kingdom he inherited and erected the temple God Himself had designed (1 Chronicles 28:11, 20), which took some seven years to complete. His own gorgeous palace, one of the wonders of the world at that time, in which scarcely anything appeared less valuable than silver and gold, was thirteen years in building. The immense store of wealth his father had reserved for the temple enabled Solomon to carry out his grandiose schemes. Such wealth speedily disappeared, resulting in the heavy taxation of the people in order to complete his magnificent whims.

As he strengthened his own kingdom, he was astute enough to form alliances with surrounding nations making possible extensive commerce in all kinds of goods. He built the first trading fleet which ventured as far as the mysterious port of Ophir which, some scholars say, was in India. Thus, the gaudy pomp and pride brought him international fame. Even Jesus referred to the glory of Solomon.

Solomon was the world's first great naturalist as his references to birds and animals, fields and flowers prove. As an author he was renowned, having written over a 1000 songs, and composed or gathered 3000 proverbs, a number of which make up the Book of Proverbs. Two other books, Ecclesiastes and the Song of Solomon also came from his pen. Alas! however, magnificence in so many fields turned to misery. A life commencing like the cloudless dawn of a summer's morning, ended in a night of sin, shame, and sorrow, as the fame of Solomon began to fade. He was wise but wicked, successful but sensual.

The cause of the fall and decline of this once mighty, autocratic ruler was women. Desiring a wife, he went to

Egypt for a queen and found her in a daughter of Pharaoh—an alliance which saddened the godly elect of Israel, for with her came her heathen gods, for which Solomon built temples. Then came the large harem of women from all parts who caused Solomon to sin, and with 700 wives and 300 concubines, such polygamy turned him into an idolater, making the temple he had built for God most nauseating to the Almighty.

Wealth, pride, and sensuality brought about the tragic deterioration of a life that began with great promise, a sad story Solomon himself wrote about in Ecclesiastes, in which he describes how all the rivers of wisdom and wealth, pomp and power, wine and women, music and song, ran into his sea, and yet he was not satisfied. He had tried everything under the sun, but all was vanity and vexation of spirit simply because of his departure from God, who is the secret Source of every precious thing. In all his popularity Solomon came to lose his piety.

Is it possible, then, to isolate any event in Solomon's life and say, "This was your finest hour"? Doubtless he himself felt he had many a noble hour as the glory of his kingdom expanded. But we think that *the finest hour* the king who reigned for forty years ever had was the one that came to him as a young man. God appeared before Solomon and said, "Ask what I shall give thee" (2 Chronicles 1:7). Then, praising the piety of his father, David, he prayed that his mantle might fall upon him, as he succeeded him as king.

Recognizing the enormous task ahead, he asked God for an understanding heart to judge His people, and to discern between good and bad. Solomon asked nothing for himself, save the impartation of a wise and an understanding heart—a wisdom he soon manifested in the case of the two harlots over a child. The plea of Solomon for wisdom, presented in all humility, so pleased God that He said, "I will give thee riches, and wealth, and honour, such as none of the kings have had that have been before thee, neither shall there any after thee have the like" (2 Chronicles 1:12).

But the sad story is that Solomon failed to discern between the good and bad in his own life, and turned to the bad, thus, prostituting the noble sentiments expressed in his prayer that he was as a little child: not knowing how to go out or come in. Later on, he was to write, "Before honour is humility" (Proverbs 15:33; 18:12), and that "By humility and the fear of the Lord are riches, and honour, and life" (Proverbs 22:4). Solomon, however, did not practice what he preached for in his rise to honor, he lost his humility. He neglected to include in his wardrobe of glittering and gorgeous kingly robes the garment of humility he clothed himself with at his installation to kingship, and consequently brought his initial hour, so full of promise, to a final hour of remorse, discontent, and self-contempt. His God-imparted wisdom was not used to teach him self-control, and he died leaving only a violated family life, and his glorious united kingdom rent by jealousy.

Wherein lies our safeguard? How imperative it is, in the light of Solomon's tragic decline to give heed to what Jesus had to say about humility:

Whosoever exalteth himself shall be abased; and he that humbleth himself shall be exalted.

Luke 14:11

Then we have the specific declarations of James:

> God resisteth the proud, but giveth grace unto the humble. Humble yourselves in the sight of the Lord, and he shall lift you up.
>
> James 4:6, 10

13

Esther and Her Fine Hour of Resolution

ONLY TWO BOOKS out of the sixty-six forming the Bible carry the names of women, namely, Ruth and Esther. Also, only two books have no mention of God in them whatever—Esther and the Song of Solomon. Yet although no divine name appears in Esther, the book has the atmosphere of the overruling providence of God, of whom Isaiah says, "Verily thou art a God that hidest thyself" (Isaiah 45:15). And He is behind and controlling the events. His finger is evident in directing the safety of His chosen people. If the unseen devil, a murderer from the beginning, put it into the heart of Haman to contrive, not only Mordecai's death, but the slaughter of the Jewish population, was it not the invisible God who put it into the heart of the king to bring about Mordecai's deliverance and honor? When sleep fled away as a shadow, as the original suggests, from Ahasuerus, was it not God who contrived his sleepless night, and suggested to his mind to call for the book of records, and learn of Mordecai's good service, resulting in his reward?

Who wrote the story of a people doomed to destruction

but remarkably delivered is not certain. A Jewish apocryphal edition has the phrase, "Then Mordecai said, God has done these things." That Mordecai was well able to relate the events of the book is proven by the letters he wrote to all the Jews regarding the peril that faced them. "Mordecai wrote these things" (Esther 9:20). The book itself has suffered much at the hands of critics, some of whom affirm that no person as Esther existed, and that the book has no historical value. Even Martin Luther was hostile to it, and wrote, "I would it did not exist, for it Judaizes too much and has in it a great deal of heathenish naughtiness. It is more worthy than all of being excluded from the Canon." We believe it to be, however, an integral part of a divinely inspired revelation.

As to Esther herself, her double name is worthy of note. Her original Hebrew name was Hadassah, meaning *a myrtle*—the myrtle plant being sweet-scented and of luxurious beauty, and, therefore, emblematic of her natural loveliness of form and countenance. Esther, her Persian name after she became queen, signifies a *star*— some writers identify as Venus, a bright luminary of wonder and admiration. The Babylonian Venus was the goddess of beauty, and used of Esther can suggest the style of beauty for which she was renowned. We are told that she was fair and beautiful and, consequently, "obtained favour in the sight of all them that looked upon her" (Esther 2:15). Left an orphan, she was reared by her cousin, Mordecai, who held a minor position among the palace officials, and he proved to be her admirable guardian and counselor. Matthew Henry says of Esther, "Her wisdom and her virtue were her greatest beauty, but it is an advantage to a diamond to be well set."

The romantic record of this orphan girl who rose to

become queen of one of the world's greatest empires, and who resolved to die in an effort to save her race from slaughter can be briefly told. Vashti, the reigning queen, who bravely refused to obey the command of her drunken husband to display herself before a drunken crowd, was deposed, and a successor sought. By subtle maneuvering, Mordecai succeeded in having Esther included among the virgins from whom the king would choose another queen, and when it came her turn to be presented, King Ahasuerus was immediately struck with her unusual posture and beauty, and loving her above all others made her queen.

Haman, who was next to the king in power, was the Jews' enemy bent on their removal from the kingdom by death. He had made undercover plans to hang Mordecai, and slay the Jews. Until this time Mordecai and Esther had hidden their Jewish descent, but when Esther learned of Haman's wicked plans she pleaded for the Jews to be spared. When Haman's plot was revealed, he was hanged on the same gallows he had prepared for Mordecai. Thus, this first great anti-Semite came to experience in a tragic way that they who cursed the Jews would be cursed of God, which brings us to the question of the finest hour in the life of Esther.

Orthodox Jews have no doubt as to her sublime hour, as their Feast of Purim indicates. The festival lasts for two days during which the Book of Esther is solemnly read, and there is much rejoicing over Queen Esther saving her race from annihilation. Esther at the time of crisis knew that she could not present her plea for the Jews unless the king invited her to approach the throne by the wave of a golden sceptre. To venture near him without such an invitation would have meant death for her. How privileged the saints are to approach the footstool of God's throne of grace *boldly!*

Esther was hesitant about placing herself where the king could see her, but Mordecai insisted that she must make the effort for if the decree had gone forth to destroy all Jews, Esther and he would be among the slain. Resolving then, whatever it cost her to apply to the king, Esther, with courage and resolution, said to Mordecai: "I will go in unto the king, which is not according to the law: and if *I perish, I perish"* (Esther 4:16, italics added). Such a sacrificial decision was not taken in despair and passion, for Esther was a Jewess who knew the God of Israel, and believed that she could trust Him with the issue of her holy resolve. Her life could not be forfeited in a nobler cause than that of saving God's people from slaughter, and so her intercession for them brought her to *her finest hour.*

14

Job and His Fine Hour of Trust

A FASCINATING FEATURE of the study of Bible characters is the variety of personality they present. No two persons are identical, as peas in a pod. Prominent figures appear with an individuality all their own. What a dreary, monotonous world it would be if we were all exactly alike! That God loves variety is seen in the manifold, different fruits and flowers, trees and plants surrounding us. Even one star differs from another in glory. When Paul declared, "By the grace of God I am what I am" (1 Corinthians 15:10), he likely had in mind his own unique identity, as well as his trials and triumphs as an apostle. John Wesley was wont to say that when God made him he broke the mold, implying that there would never be another like him.

It is with this common, characteristic individuality before us that we note the evident disparity between the character of Solomon and that of Job, whom we are now dealing with and who are as much alike as cheese and chalk. Job had abundant possessions at the beginning, lost them but not his faith in God, and at the end had twice as much as he started out with. Solomon began life richly endowed, but ended in misery with his kingdom tragically divided. In spite of all he had possessed and lost, Job retained his humility; but Solomon became proud, parted with his earlier humbleness of heart, and suffered the withdrawal of divine favor. What a rich observation that was that Bacon made, when he wrote, "The pencil of the Holy Ghost hath laboured more in describing the afflictions of Job than the felicities of Solomon." May ours be the undying passion to serve Christ our Redeemer to the utmost of our own capacity and personality!

The critics of Scripture have a heyday with the Book of Job, many of whom deny that there was such a person who lived in the Land of Uz. We have no hesitation in accepting this Book as true history, and Job, as an actual person, we expect to meet in heaven. In 2 King Henry IV (1.2.145), Shakespeare makes one of his characters say, "I am as poor as Job, my lord, but not so patient."

Pertinent facts about Job, in the Godward and selfward aspects of his life are clearly defined for us in this dramatic book. He was perfect and upright, feared God and shunned evil. No other man in Scripture is spoken of as being "perfect." He had a wife, seven sons, and three daughters for whom he manifested spiritual concern. He was a very wealthy landowner, possessing 7,000 sheep, 500 she-asses, and required many servants in his household to assist him. He must have had widespread moral influence, as he was reckoned to be the greatest of all men in the East. He had friends, four of whom are named, who were not as kind and understanding as they were candid. At the end of his long season of trial, God vindicated Job before his friends, and rebuked them for not saying the things that were right. Then we have a precious touch.

Job "prayed for his friends" (Job 42:10), Eliphaz, Bildad, Zophar, and Elihu, who doubtless became truer friends as the result of this. Yes, Job also had his foes, Satan himself, the Sabeans and Chaldeans, and the great wilderness wind that stripped him of flocks and brought death to his servants.

To search for a fine hour in a life so sorely tried may seem to be a hopeless task, although some might indicate that Job came to his finest hour when God made up all his losses and gave him twice as much as he had before calamity left him naked. But his most sublime hours came when, in spite of all his trials and tribulations, he ever spoke that which was right concerning God, who permitted the satanic testing of him (Job 2:1–8).

It was a fine hour when he did not charge God foolishly for the loss of lives and possessions, but said, "The Lord gave, and the Lord hath taken away; blessed be the name of the Lord" (Job 1:21).

It was, perhaps, *his finest hour* of all when his own wife urged him to abandon his integrity, and "curse God, and die" (Job 2:9). Although he loved the one who had given him ten children, he was forthright in his reply, "Thou speakest as one of the foolish women speaketh. What? shall we receive good at the hand of God, and shall we not receive evil?" (Job 2:10). Job retained his integrity for he did not sin with his lips.

It was another fine hour when, scorned by his friends, Job poured out his tears to God, and said, "O that one might plead for a man with God, as a man pleadeth for his neighbour!" (Job 16:21). How he wanted a daysman, between God and himself to mediate. Through grace, the Christian has a Daysman in Jesus, the Mediator, who lays his hand upon God and himself, forming an eternal union thereby.

It was a further sublime hour when he magnificently defended God in his reply to his friends who came to think of him as hypocrite and a liar, and declared in the midst of his extreme physical afflictions, "Though he slay me, yet will I trust in him" (Job 13:15). We could take this as the key verse of the entire Book; and also a foregleam of the cry from the Cross, "Why didst thou forsake me?"

It was surely a most glorious hour in Job's experience when, forgotten by familiar friends, turned against by his wife and children, and enduring terrible physical ailments, he could give the world such a wonderful testament of faith in imperishable words:

> I know that my redeemer liveth, and that he shall stand at the latter day upon the earth: And though after my skin worms destroy this body, yet in my flesh shall I see God; Whom I shall see for myself, and mine eyes shall behold, and not another; though my veins be consumed within me.
>
> Job 19:25–27

In the depth of his darkness and agony of his suffering, Job held on to God and was upheld by God. It pleased the Lord, for a wise purpose, to bruise this perfect man who feared Him. Because he was a righteous man who shunned evil, his sufferings were not due to any sins of his own, but were permitted by a loving and just God to exhibit the strength of trust and patience in hours of the sorest trials. Thus, after he was tried, Job came out of the furnace of affliction as gold. Amid all our tribulation, losses, and crosses, Job has left us the example, of having our eyes and heart ever toward the Lord, praying:

He knoweth the way that I take: when he hath tried me,
I shall come forth as gold. My foot hath held his steps,
his way have I kept, and not declined.

Job 23:10, 11

No wonder at the end of Job's long Gethsemane, God
gave him double for all that he had lost in his hours of
anguish.

15

Isaiah and His Fine Hour of Vision

In 3 King Henry VI (2.5.26), Shakespeare asks, "How many make the hour full complete?" We are now to consider a famous saint of old who did make his fine hour "full complete." With the Book of Isaiah, with its sixty-six chapters, a miniature of the Bible with its sixty-six books, we pass from poetry into prophecy, and are introduced into one of the most important sections of the Word. Isaiah was by no means the first prophet of the sixteen following him, but is placed first because his prophecy is the largest of them all, and records most of Immanuel, to whom all the prophets gave witness. This is why some of the ancients referred to Isaiah as *the Evangelical Prophet,* and as *a Fifth Evangelist.*

Before the Word of God was printed, the prophets, because of their privileged intimacy with heaven, and, therefore, commanding authority on earth, "were as Bibles to the Church." Under the Spirit of God, these messengers exercised their own personal and particular genius, and thus were not merely speaking trumpets through whom the Spirit spoke, "but speaking men *by* whom the Spirit spoke, making use of their natural powers, in respect both of light and flame, and advancing them above themselves," as F. B. Meyer reminds us. This fact is clearly evident in the prophet before us who, according to Jewish tradition, was of a royal family, his father, Amos, being brother to King Uzziah. Isaiah's wife was a prophetess.

Coming to the New Testament, we find that more of Isaiah's prophecies, particularly concerning Christ, are quoted, than those of any other prophet. While we think of him primarily as a prophet, he was also a poet of no mean order (Isaiah 1:3; 5:18; 12:1–6; 13:2). No other Old Testament writer uses so many beautiful and picturesque epigrams and metaphors as Isaiah, the preacher of righteousness. This first and most prominent of Israel's prophets had two sons, who were given names symbolic of aspects conspicuous of the nation's history at the time Isaiah uttered his predictions. The name of one was Shearjashub, meaning *a remnant shall return;* and the other was known by the long name of Mahershalalhashbaz, implying, *Haste ye, speed to the spoil.*

This dreamer and poet, architect and builder, theologian and saint, was an orator without peer, so much so, that Jerome likened him to Demosthenes, the Athenian orator of the third century B.C. Stern in tone, he was also tender and compassionate, and as an artist with words, used language that stirred the hearts of men. Nothing is known of the death of Isaiah. Legend records that he was finally placed inside a hollow tree and sawn asunder at the command of Manasseh because of his prophecy against this evil man (Hebrews 11:37).

It is an easy task to go through the Book of this chiefest of the writing prophets and select many fine hours, "full complete," that Isaiah experienced during his long and divinely blessed ministry. What a great hour that must have been when he prophesied that, "a virgin shall conceive, and bear a son, and shall call his name Immanuel" (Isaiah 7:14), a sign that was fulfilled when the Virgin Mary gave birth to Jesus. Then, what another fine and heart-stirring hour that must have been for the prophet when he further revealed the full names and mission of the One to be born of a virgin. As a child, He would be born of a woman, but as a Son He would come as a gift from God. "His name [not names] shall be called Wonderful, Counsellor, The mighty God, The everlasting Father, The Prince of Peace. Of the increase of his government and peace there shall be no end" (Isaiah 9:6, 7).

Further, many Bible lovers doubtless reckon the hour eclipsing all others in Isaiah's life and ministry was when he testified beforehand the sufferings of Christ and the glory that should follow in his prophecy that drips with the ruby blood of the Redeemer. Nowhere else in the Old Testament have we such a full prophecy of the death and resurrection of Jesus as found in Isaiah 53—a chapter so "replenished with the unsearchable riches of Christ that it may be called rather the Gospel of the evangelist Isaiah than the prophecy of the Prophet Isaiah," to quote Dr. Meyer again.

While other visions and prophecies might be cited as constituting the prophet's fine hours during his ministry, personally, I select, Isaiah 6, as being the finest hour that came to the prophet who gave us the cameo of Jesus as *The Man of Sorrows*. Although Isaiah's call to service is not recorded, the opening chapter of his prophecy suggests a tacit commission to function as a prophet. In chapter six, however, we have a vision with its definite call to service—a commission from the Lord, Isaiah never failed in fulfilling. Such a distinct call established his faith, and nerved him to serve the Lord with zeal and faithfulness. This remarkable vision has a threefold aspect:

> It was a vision of a Throne and of its royal Occupant (1–4).
> It was a vision of a Heart in need of cleansing (5–7).
> It was a vision of a Sphere awaiting the prepared prophet (8–13).

Such an overwhelming manifestation came to Isaiah when King Uzziah died, and emphasis is on the little word *also* in the opening verse, for he saw, not only a tomb but a throne, not only a grave but glory. The famous king of Israel who reigned for fifty years was dead, but Israel's God still lived. The unfortunate king died as a leper in a leper house, but the King, the Lord of Hosts, was in His temple, high and lifted up, from the sicknesses and death of humans. Uzziah went to his grave alone, but the Lord on His majestic throne had the seraphim, an angelic host expressive of the divine holiness of the deathless King Isaiah saw, and who was, "Holy, Holy, Holy" (Isaiah 6:3). Uzziah's throne had been emptied by his death, but the Throne in Glory is never vacant for its Occupant is One upon whom death has no hold.

But the reflexive influence of such a glorious vision of sovereignty was not what Isaiah expected. We can imagine him saying, *I never expected such a heavenly vision to reveal my vileness. I should have been elated in seeing my Lord's glory, and go forth to serve Him in the strength of it, but instead I see my guilt.* So we have the cry "Woe is me!

for I am undone: because I am a man of unclean lips"
(Isaiah 6:5).

The prophet's grief over his personal sin was increased
by the realization that all around him suffered from the
same scourge for he dwelt among those who were "a
people of unclean lips." With the discovery of our own
heart's need, there always follows a clearer vision of the
guilt of a lost world. But for *each* and *all*, there is the
cleansing fire. A messenger from the Throne silenced the
prophet's fears by assuring him that, as the result of the
fire from off the altar, his iniquity was removed, and his
sin purged. For our hearts, in this age of grace, we have
the assurance that the blood of Jesus is able to cleanse us
from all sin.

From the vision of a *Throne,* and of a *Heart,* we now
turn to the vision of a *Sphere.* The full blaze of
sovereignty, producing salvation, resulted in service. The
Lord must be seen in His glory and grace, before He can
be served. It is perfectly true that we are saved to serve,
but it is equally true that we cannot serve the Lord effectively unless we are saved. David, in his penitential
Psalm, recognized the right order when he prayed,
"Purge me with hyssop, and I shall be clean . . . . Then
[and not till *then*] will I teach transgressors thy ways; and
sinners shall be converted unto thee" (Psalms 51:7, 13).
Paul has the same sequence in his greeting to Timothy,
his spiritual son, "[God] Who hath saved us, and called us
with an holy calling" (2 Timothy 1:9). Conversion must
always precede the call.

As to Isaiah's commission, the sphere he was to occupy,
seems to be out of harmony with the double vision of the
King's glory and grace just received. We would have

thought that after such a revelation, the prophet would have been thrust forth as a flaming evangelist turning multitudes to the Lord of Hosts. But, evidently, such a soul-absorbing vision of a Sovereign Redeemer was to fit Isaiah for a strange mission; namely, to foretell the ruin of his people and even to ripen for such a ruin because of their utter rejection of God. Responding to the divine call, "Whom shall I send, and who will go for us?" Isaiah immediately answered, "Here am I: send me" (Isaiah 6:8). But did he know where he was to be sent? The verses covering the prophet's painful commission are quoted in part, or referred to, six times in the New Testament, as a warning to those of any age who willfully reject the revelation of God.

It was a hard task for Isaiah to proclaim a message that would result in the hardening of sinners, rather than turning them to the Lord, but difficult spheres are not easily filled, and those who occupy them must have the deep, spiritual upheaval in heart and life the prophet experienced if they are to face what seems to be a hopeless situation. In the main, the prophecy of Isaiah was denunciatory, yet he had an encouraging message for the godly remnant, remaining true to Him whose train filled the temple. How precious, then, are the lessons we can learn from Isaiah's *finest hour!*

Ezekiel is another of the major prophets we would like to deal more fully with if space permitted, but a brief paragraph must suffice. Like his fellow-prophet Isaiah, Ezekiel was also a priest and a prophet, and similarly proclaimed a message of judgment and denounced false prophets. Donald Fraser said of him, "Even when the understanding is puzzled, the heart burns inwardly at the recital of Ezekiel's visions and those burdens which the

Lord laid upon his spirit." The prophet was happy in his homelife, but the hour came when God revealed to him that his beloved wife, the desire of his eyes, would die of a sudden sickness, and that he was not to weep, mourn, or fast, or allow any public lamentation for one so dear. Ezekiel's *finest hour* came as he obeyed the hard command of God for we read that "at even my wife died: and I did in the morning as I was commanded" (Ezekiel 24:18). Previously, he had said to the people, "I am your sign" (Ezekiel 12:11), and Ezekiel's sore anguish was to serve as a sign that Jerusalem would be destroyed because of its gross sin without wailing or lamentations.

Hosea is another of the Prophets whose sad story we could linger over. Described as "the first prophet of Grace and Israel's earliest evangelist," Hosea had a very heavy heart because of the iniquities and idolatries of the Northern Kingdom of which he was part. He has also earned the title of "The Prophet of a Sorrowful Heart" because of his tragic homelife. Gomer, Hosea's wife, became unfaithful, and the accounts of his marriage, children, and his wife's degeneracy make sad reading. God told him to take a wife of whoredoms, which he did and had sons by her, and they became signs of divine judgments upon Israel.

The prophet's *finest hour* came when, amid his personal anguish over his wife's immorality, he went forth to declare God's sorrow over His unfaithful people and manifested through his broken heart the character of God. Israel had had a long history of leaving God, as Gomer had left Hosea for other lovers, and so the prophet came to see in his own suffering a reflection of the heart of God amid Israel's unfaithfulness. But it must have been a blissful hour when the erring wife returned, the price of her redemption being paid by Hosea himself. Thus he became a sign of divine grace, reflecting God's character, foreshadowing the ultimate redemption through the Messiah and Israel's redemption as a nation. Hosea's hour of personal suffering brought him into sympathy with the heart of God, and such a result always constitutes the *finest hour* for the sufferer.

16

Daniel and the Three Hebrew Youths and Their Fine Hour of Defiance

JOHN DRYDEN, expressive poet of the latter part of the seventeenth century, described those who "like sentries, are obliged to stand . . . and wait the 'pointed hour." In the fascinating Book of Daniel we have the record of those who, standing sentry-like, awaited their 'pointed hour of decreed martyrdom, but who came to realize that it was their glorious hour of miraculous deliverance. The Book itself with its visions and dreams, with both historical and prophetical chapters comprising it, is easy to read.

Daniel himself, whom the ancient historian Flavius Josephus called one of the "greatest of the prophets," possessed a double name, the Chaldean one being Belteshazzar meaning, either, *One who lays up in secret* or *he that secretly endures pain and pressure*. Daniel signifies *the judgment of God* or *God is my judge*. Descended from the royal family of David, Daniel was carried captive to Babylon as a child, but became a prophet eminent for wisdom and piety. Ezekiel refers to his superior wisdom (Ezekiel 28:3). In a foreign land, Daniel became active in the life of the courts and councils of some of the greatest monarchs, such as Nebuchadnezzar, Cyrus, and Darius. Coming from a royal family, he lived like a prince and became a prime minister, courtier, an official of kings, and a conspicuous man of business. Close intimacy with heaven made him a divine interpreter of visions and dreams, and the renowned prophet of Gentile dominion and defeat. Bishop Ken, hymn writer of the sixteenth century, wrote of him, "Daniel was one that kept his station in the greatest of revolutions, reconciling politics and religion, business and devotion, magnanimity with humility, authority with affability, conversation with retirement, Heaven and the Court, the favour of God and of the King."

From the opening chapter of his story we gather that he was handsome and had a princely air about him. One of the traditions about Daniel says that "he had a spare, dry tall figure with a beautiful expression." The high sculpture of his life is emphasized by Alexander Whyte in his *Bible Characters.* "There is always a singular lustre and nobility and stately distinction about him. There is a note of birth and breeding and aristocracy about his whole name and character." Our main objective in this chapter is to indicate the finest hour that came to Daniel and the three Hebrew youths, all of whom were brought as captives to Babylon from Jerusalem, and all of whom were youths "in whom was no blemish, but well favoured, and skilful in all wisdom, and cunning in knowledge, and understanding science, and such as had ability in them to stand in the king's palace, and whom they might teach the learning and the tongue of the Chaldeans" (Daniel 1:4).

The original names of the three youths were Hananiah, Mishael, and Azariah, but as with Daniel, these were changed to Shadrach, Meshach, and Abednego—all three figuring conspicuously in King Nebuchadnezzar's pride and punishment as recorded in chapter three, where they are specifically mentioned by name thirteen times. Daniel, and his three companions were all consigned to a terrible death from which they were divinely preserved.

King Nebuchadnezzar had a dream that greatly troubled him, but he could not remember its details. The command went out for magicians, astrologers, and sorcerers to come to the palace and recount the dream, and give its interpretation. Offers of a rich reward awaited those who could interpret the dream. But the wise men stated how impossible it was for any man on earth to do as the king wished. "There is none other that can shew it before the king, except the gods, whose dwelling is not with flesh" (Daniel 2:11).

Infuriated at such a failure, the king issued a decree that all wise men, including Daniel and his three companions, should be slain. Daniel, learning of the death decree, came before the king and told him that the God of heaven who dwelt with, and used, sanctified flesh would reveal the substance and interpretation of his dream. In a night vision the miracle happened. Daniel received the secret of it all from God, went to the king with the revelation, and he was made to realize that the interpretation was all of God. As the result of this monarchy vision, the king received a panorama of the course, character, and consummation of the Gentile Age, with Nebuchadnezzar himself becoming the ruler of the first world empire.

Daniel was worshiped and rewarded by the king, as were his three companions. Then came the admission of the king that the four Hebrews served a God, who was the God of gods, and a revealer of secrets. But puffed up with pride over his elevation as a world ruler, Nebuchadnezzar set up a golden image of himself, and commanded all the Chaldeans to fall down and worship the image, with the threat that all who failed to do so would be cast into a burning fiery furnace. It was thus that Shadrach, Meshach, and Abednego came to their finest hour—and what a great hour it was.

The king personally urged the youths to obey his decree with the ultimatum, "Who is that God that shall deliver you out of my hands?" Evidently he had forgotten his previous declaration that the God they worshiped was the God of gods, the Lord of lords. Defiantly, the three answered that if the God they served did not deliver them, then they were ready to perish in the flames. Here is their courageous refusal to obey Nebuchadnezzar.

> If it be so, our God whom we serve is able to deliver us from the burning fiery furnace, and he will deliver us out of thine hand, O king. But if not, be it known unto thee, O king, that we will not serve thy gods, nor worship the golden image which thou hast set up.
>
> Daniel 3:17, 18

Down through the centuries, it has been ever thought, *This was their finest hour*. We all know the sequel. Stirred with anger at such a defiant answer, the king ordered the furnace to be heated seven times more than it was wont to be heated, and bound and fully clothed to make death more horrible, they were cast into the flames which were so intense that the attendants responsible for throwing them in were scorched to death.

The three youths, who were walking around, still clothed and no longer bound, were acting as if they were strolling around on a warm, sunny day. But the secret of their deliverance was the presence of another, a fourth person whose form was "like the Son of God" (v. 25). He, it was who fulfilled the promise on behalf of the brave godly young men:

> When thou walkest through the fire, thou shalt not be burned; neither shall the flame kindle upon thee.
>
> Isaiah 43:2

Even Nebuchadnezzar had to confess when the youths walked out of the furnace, "There is no other God that can deliver after this sort" (Daniel 3:29). Their bodies had been yielded to death, because of their trust in God, and for such a willing sacrifice, the king abundantly rewarded them. The message for our own hearts from this story of those who would rather suffer than sin is expressed for us by Matthew Henry, "Those that suffer for Christ have his gracious presence with them in their sufferings, even in the fiery furnace, even in the valley of the shadow of death, and therefore even there they need *fear no evil*." Many a saint has reached their finest hour in the furnace of affliction.

One cannot think of Daniel without recalling Joseph. Both were taken as captives in their youth to a foreign country. Both suffered for righteousness' sake but were victorious. Both rose to great eminence in the land of their captivity. To many Bible lovers, Daniel is their favorite Old Testament character because of his colorful career. In the earlier days of his captivity in Babylon, he determined not to defile himself with the king's meat; and, after he rose to prominence was just as determined not to obey a king's royal edict which was against his conscience.

What we have chosen as Daniel's finest hour is his witness before King Darius in chapter six. Because the king preferred Daniel above the presidents and princes of his realm because of the prophet's excellent spirit, he decided to make him prime minister of the state. But the presidents and princes who could not find "any error or fault" in Daniel's life, decided to attack his Godward bent. So they came to the king with a proposition that he should make a statute prohibiting any person asking a petition of any God or man for thirty days, save of the king himself. The penalty for disobeying would be death in a lion's den. Daniel knew that this was an endeavor to interfere with his prayer life.

But Daniel flouted the decree, went into his house, and, with the windows opened toward Jerusalem where he had first learned to pray, he knelt and prayed and praised God, three times a day. With the windows open, all could see him at prayer, as did the presidents and princes who were so jealous of him. They found Daniel praying and making supplication before his God, and told the king of Daniel's defiance of the statute, which, because of the law of the Medes and Persians, could not be changed. What else could the king do but cast him into the den of lions? But Darius knew Daniel to be a man of God, and although he committed him to a probable death, he made the remarkable statement, "Thy God whom thou servest continually, he will deliver thee" (Daniel 6:16). Do you not think that this was Daniel's *finest hour?*

During Daniel's first night among the lions, no harm befell simply because God, in response to His courageous, defiant servant, had "stopped the mouths of lions" (Hebrews 11:33). But with Darius it was different. While Daniel likely slept well, warmed by his animal companions, the king spent a melancholy, sleepless night. "Sleep went from him." With the dawn, he hastened to the den and cried with a lamentable voice, "O Daniel, servant of the living God, is thy God, whom thou servest continually able to deliver thee from the lions?" What a fine hour it was when Daniel, alive, safe, and unharmed presented himself, and without any reproach, welcomed the king with the salutation, "O king, live for ever" (Daniel 6:18–21).

Daniel's life had been spared by a miracle, and he immediately gave His praise for his preservation from death. The "angel" he mentioned was the same one seen in "the form of the Son of God," who had delivered Daniel's three companions in the fiery furnace. Having "believed in his God," the prophet proved Him to be the God of deliverances, to which Darius gave witness in his decree to all his people to tremble and fear before the God of Daniel, even the God who had delivered him from the power of the lions. As for those who had engineered Daniel's committal to the den of lions, purely out of spite because of his integrity, they were taken along with their families and consigned to the same den only to find that the mouths of the lions were no longer shut, but wide open to destroy the accusers. Thus, they suffered the punishment they had designed for Daniel, who as the result of his hour of trial and yet vindication, was promoted to still greater office in the land to which he had been brought as an exile. The hymn would have us join "Daniel's band":

> *Standing by a purpose true,*
> *Heeding God's command,*
> *Honor them, the faithful few!*
> *All hail to Daniel's band!*
>
> P. P. BLISS

17

John the Baptist and His Fine Hour of Condemnation

As we take up the coverage of the fine hours many New Testament notable figures experienced, a word is necessary concerning the long gap between the Old and New Testaments, sometimes called *The Silent Years*. This darkest period in the history of Israel spanned some 400 years, and as we have no scriptural information of this historical era, we are dependent upon the works of Josephus, the Jewish historian, who lived about that time, and also several apocryphal records. A satisfying synopsis of this period can be found in the Scofield Reference Bible. During the time of Israel's spiritual declension, dynasties changed six times, namely, Persian, Alexandrian, Egyptian, Syrian, Maccabean, and Roman. Yet amid the trials of God's people, and their departure from His revealed Word, there was a remnant who waited for redemption in Jerusalem, as the longing of Anna the prophetess proves.

Chapter 3 of the Book of Matthew opens with the life and ministry of John the Baptist, whose coming to introduce better days for Israel, was prophesied by Malachi, as the Old Testament ended and the intertestament began. The prophet, who was given a revelation of the coming Messiah, also foretold the advent of His forerunner, John the Baptist, in the declaration from God—"Behold, I will send my messenger, and he shall prepare the way before me"—a prophecy which Jesus, when He appeared, applied to the Baptist (Malachi 3:1; Matthew 11:10). That he followed the goodly fellowship of Old Testament prophets is evident from our Lord's high estimation of His remarkable forerunner:

> What went ye out into the wilderness to see? . . . A prophet? yea, I say unto you, and more than a prophet . . . Verily I say unto you, Among them that are born of women there hath not risen a greater than John the Baptist.
>
> Matthew 11:7–11

And thus, it is, that standing at the open door of the New Testament is the dominant figure of the Baptist as the foreclosure of one era and the forerunner of a new era, and ready to make the transition from law to grace as he proclaimed the Messiah as the Lamb of God who would bear away the sin of the world. Born of godly Zacharias and Elisabeth, as a child of promise, the miraculous was associated with his birth for his parents were old and Elisabeth was long past the age of having children, yet God declared that they would have a son, and that his name was to be called John.

But if John came into the world as the result of a miracle, no miracle was performed to save him at the end of his mission from a brutal death. And in this he resembled the Lamb he proclaimed, for Jesus had a miraculous

birth—a virgin birth—but there was no miracle to prevent
His bitter and shameful death on a cross. Much as we
would like to give a fuller exposition of this rugged
character in the Bible's portrait gallery, we must content
ourselves with one or two brief facts.

First of all, John was a man of the desert, with his as-
cetic affinities who knew how to practice self-denial, and
was spare of diet and clothing. Through his abstentions
he developed self-reliance and spiritual strength in com-
munion with God in the desert solitudes he loved. We
read that he "was in the deserts till the day of his shewing
unto Israel" (Luke 1:80).

In his varied career, there were many outstanding and
momentous hours. Doubtless many diligent Bible readers
would choose John's baptism of Jesus, as his greatest and
finest hour, and this was certainly a much-honored privilege, and one from which he sincerely shrank. But his
Lord said, "Suffer it to be so," and with His baptism the
heavens opened and the Holy Spirit descended and a
voice from heaven said, "Thou art my beloved Son; in
thee I am well pleased" (Luke 3:22).

Our preference of the Baptist's finest hour, however,
came when he confronted King Herod, and reproved him
to his face, for all the evils he had done. The most glaring
sin he condemned the tetrarch of was that of living with
his brother's wife, and without apology he said to the
ruler, "It is not lawful for thee to have her" (Matthew
14:4). John showed no fear or timidity in his condemnation. He did not water down the accusation by saying, "I
don't like to say this, Your Majesty, and I am sorry to have
to say it, but really you should not be living with a woman
who is already married to another." Preachers, who
preach what the Bible stoutly condemns, in an apologetic

fashion, are not worth their salt. John had no need to be afraid of Herod for Herod feared John, knowing that he was a just and holy man.

When John troubled the conscience of the sinning Herod, he reached *his finest hour,* even though it was an hour that led to his martyrdom—a cruel death Herodias, the woman Herod had no right to be living with, cunningly engineered. Herod also made a promise he should not have made in his muddled state of mind—the result of too much wine at his birthday banquet. He became exceeding sorry, at the death of John which, for his oath's sake, he felt was imperative. Had he had any just manhood about him he should have broken his oath, and sent the licentious Herodias back to her lawful husband. It was the passion-raising dancing of the daughter of Herodias that resulted in the Baptist's noble head being severed from his body, and, as C. H. Spurgeon aptly put it, "John was the first Baptist minister to lose his head through dancing."

18

Matthew and His Fine Hour of Renunciation

A STRIKING FEATURE of the Old Testament is the way its opening and closing verses summarize its tragic history. It begins with the name *GOD*; and ends with the word *curse*; and the record reveals how man came under the curse of the law because of his disobedience to, and rejection of, His will and Word. But with the New Testament it is totally different for it begins with the name *JESUS*; and ends with a benediction: "The grace of our Lord Jesus Christ be with you all" (Genesis 1:1; Malachi 4:6; Matthew 1:1; Revelation 22:21). *Law—Grace!* The Gospel Matthew wrote proclaims that Jesus was born the Saviour, and that, through all He would accomplish, the sinner would be forever redeemed, by matchless grace, from the curse and load of sin. In his own spiritual experience, Matthew became a trophy of such a blood-bought emancipation. It is to this disciple that we owe the blessed message, "Thou shalt call his name JESUS; for he shall save his people from their sins" (Matthew 1:21).

The prominent character of Matthew's Gospel is the appearance of the convenanted King, promised in the Old

Testament, and the agenda of His kingdom. Thus, in his genealogy of Jesus Christ, he begins by stating that He came as the "son of David, the son of Abraham," implying that He came as *the* King, of which David was a type; and as the One obedient unto death of which Abraham in the surrender of Isaac was also a type. In his concluding chapters 26–28, Matthew gives us a detailed account of the sacrificial death of Jesus as the Son of Abraham. While writing for Israel, and the salvation she could expect as "His people" from their sins, Matthew, likewise, proclaims the Gospel of Redemption for the whole world through the coming of Jesus Christ—"Go ye therefore, and teach all nations" (Matthew 28:19).

Of Matthew himself nothing is recorded of his previous life apart from the fact that he was the son of Alphaeus. He was another Hebrew with a double name, the original one being Levi, meaning *joined,* and as first used by the Levites implied one joined unto the Lord. But in his despised occupation, Matthew prostituted his given name at birth and became joined to the world's crooked, extortionate ways and mercenary aims, for his vocation was that of a tax-gatherer for the hated foreign power, Rome, under whose yoke orthodox Jews chafed.

These collectors of taxes were usually minor officials ready to undertake their odious task among their own countrymen. Their reward was that they could extort and extract for their own benefit more tax than was due, so long as this crooked practice did not lead to revolt. This was why the publicans, as a clan, were known as leeches, since they sucked money for themselves in the process of gathering taxes for Roman emperors. It was because of their obnoxious craft that they were reckoned to be outside the pale of decent society, and in Levi's case, he was a Jew and despised by fellow Jews, as being unfit to enter the synagogue.

But the changed name, Matthew, implying *the gift of God*, suggests a changed life. Whether Levi chose it himself or Jesus coined it for him as an evidence of the transformation that had taken place we do not know. What was evident is the fact that Matthew was like the One who had called him, namely, a gift of God to Israel and to the world, which happened when the tax-gatherer came to what must have been the finest hour of his life—when he came face-to-face with Jesus. Strange though it may seem, the fullest account of what took place when the two met is given, not by Matthew himself, but by Mark (2:13–20). While we have no record of the two meeting before, Alexander Whyte, in his *Bible Characters*, says:

> Jesus of Nazareth, the carpenter's Son, knew Matthew the publican quite well. Perhaps only too well. Jesus and His mother had by this time migrated from Nazareth to Capernaum. He had often been in Matthew's toll-booth with His mother's taxes, with other poor people's taxes.

When Jesus entered His public ministry, however, He met Matthew on a different level—as the Saviour seeking a lost sinner. It is interesting to note that when Luke refers to Jesus eating and drinking with publicans and sinners, that He went on immediately to give His parables of the lost sheep, lost coin, and lost son. An eighteenth century poet wrote that:

> *One crowded hour of glorious life*
> *Is worth an age without a name.*

Our introduction to Matthew in the First Gospel brings us to a crowded hour in his nefarious business that led to a transformed, glorious life. In His journey one day after healing the sick and diseased, Jesus came to where Matthew—whom He knew as Levi—was sitting at the receipt of custom, and simply said, *Follow Me.* He did not upbraid this sinner, and expose the degrading character of his craft, pointing out its injustice in the plunder of poor people. Jesus simply called Levi to a more worthwhile occupation, namely, to serve Him rather than Caesar, and without a moment's hesitation Matthew responded to the call and came to his finest hour of renunciation for "he left all," to become the disciple of Jesus.

Luke added these three simple words *he left all* in the account of Levi's conversion and call, and what a wealth of meaning the phrase implies (Luke 5:28). There were no reserves, no half measures, no desire to hold on to some treasured side of his past life—the renunciation was complete. He left all for Him who left all in glory to become the Saviour of lost sinners, and willingly, unreserving arose from his desk, and followed Jesus. To commemorate his full surrender to Jesus, Matthew entertained Him and His disciples and many of his fellow publicans and sinners to a feast in his house, as a token of his heartfelt gratitude for his deliverance from such a sordid and sinful occupation. Also his hospitality revealed a missionary spirit, for it gave him the opportunity of introducing his old associates to Jesus in the hope that they, too, would experience that He was the Man who received sinners. There can be no doubt that contact with Jesus was *the finest hour* in Matthew's life, as it was in my own well over three quarters of a century ago, when I was charmed by the same voice divine, saying, *Follow Me!*

What Matthew did not leave behind in his renunciation were his pen and ink bottle, for growing in grace and in the knowledge of Jesus, he became, not only an apostle, but the writer of the First Gospel with its undying message of his Lord and of His image as it fell upon his own heart. As his dominant theme became *The King and His Kingdom*, Matthew alone gives us the Parables of the Kingdom. With a knowledge of Jewish life and religion, a love of truth, and a deep experience of the misery of man and the mercy of God, with self-effacing humility, he lost sight of himself in his love and adoration for the Friend of publicans and sinners for whom he had left all.

19

The Nobleman and His Fine Hour of Faith

THE FIRST TWO MIRACLES Jesus performed in Cana of Galilee after the commencement of His public ministry, offer some interesting comparisons and contrasts. The first was associated with a marriage feast, at which He turned water into wine—the second with an anxious home, in which was a son sick unto death. The first miracle speaks of joy, the second, of sorrow. At the first Jesus added much gladness to the marriage—the second, He banished sadness from the hearts of many in the Galilean home. Further, Jesus Himself must have had deep feelings as He returned to the place where he performed the first miracle that "manifested forth His glory," and caused "his disciples to believe on him" (John 2:11). John's literary touch "where he made the water wine" is characteristic of his ability to identify a place or person by some single circumstance conspicuous in an incident that occurred there.

In Samaria, where Jesus met the woman at the well, and, in the conversation about drawing water, revealed her past five marriages and her present life with a man she was not married to, there came her honest confession to the Samaritans, "Come, see a man, which told me all things that ever I did: is not this the Christ?" (John 4:29). As the result of this testimony, many of the Samaritans believed on Jesus, and begged Him to stay with them for another two days, which He did, and as an outcome, "many more believed because of his own word" (John 4:41)—not just the word of the woman. Then He journeyed from sympathetic Samaria to unsympathetic Galilee, in which He was to have mixed experiences. The miracle of the healing of the nobleman's son was one of the most encouraging episodes throughout Galilee.

John is the only writer to record this second miracle of Jesus, and he was careful to avoid much that the first three evangelists had to say about the ministry of his Lord. As news of His miracles traveled fast, the Capernaum nobleman heard of them and traveled to Cana to solicit the ministry of the Miracle Worker on behalf of his son, who was at death's door. This distressed father was indeed a *noble*man. Shakespeare has the phrase, "Live cleanly, as a nobleman should do." The word nobleman itself means one *belonging to a king,* or *well-born.* This official attached to the court of Herod Antipas, from Cana answered to all his name suggested, and must have had a spark of faith within to constrain him to attract the Healer to his distressed home.

It was pointed out that in His healing miracles Jesus strove to call out faith on the part of those who sought His aid, and that His miracles were not the cause of faith, but as the reward of such. He also knew how to draw a weak faith into stronger faith, as He did in the miracle before us. The plight of his son was the nobleman's birth pang of faith, but he revealed the limit of his faith when he limited the power of Jesus to His local presence. "Come down [to my home] ere my child die" (John 4:49). Detecting the weak point of the anxious father's faith, Jesus nurtured it, for faith, even though weak, brings relief because it is not the faith itself that relieves, but the power of the One in whom faith is placed.

Emerson in his *Essays* says, "To fill the hour—that is happiness," and the nobleman came to fill an hour with faith, and found happiness. He reached his finest hour when he realized that Jesus was able to heal by remote control, even though the distance between Capernaum and Cana was some twenty miles. So it was that, by the exercise of His will and the word of His mouth, the dying boy, miles away, was healed, for the "fever left him" as soon as His majestic lips spoke the words, "Go thy way: thy son liveth." The anxious father immediately "believed the word that Jesus had spoken, and he went his way" (John 4:50). The nobleman had found the *rest* of faith, and, believing, made no great haste to reach home to discover whether the miracle had happened.

On the way home, his servants met him with the joyful news that his dear son was alive and well, and he learned from them that the sudden change for the better came at the exact time Jesus had said, "Thy son liveth." This fact further strengthened the father's faith, and the miracle resulted in his whole household becoming believers. Nothing else could have induced them to turn to Jesus than the miracle performed in the *nobleman's finest hour*.

20

The Centurion and His Fine Hour of Modesty

WE ARE DEALING with the miracle of the healing of the centurion's servant at this point, because of the error of confusing it with the miracle just considered, the healing of the nobleman's son. Both miracles agree in revealing that Jesus was able to cure from a distance and in the absence of the sufferers, through the medium of a word. Otherwise the two miracles are totally different as the applicants themselves and those they sought healing for. We are not given different versions of the same miracle, but two distinct miracles—a distinction many scholars have drawn attention to, particularly Charles J. Ellicott, who gives us the following points of difference.

1. The nobleman pleaded for his *son*—the centurion for his *servant*, Matthew 8:16; 7:2; John 4:46.
2. The nobleman pleaded in *person*—the *elders* of the Jews interceded for the centurion, Luke 7:3; John 4:49.
3. The nobleman was a *Jew*—the centurion a *Gentile*, Luke 7:9.

4. The nobleman heard the words of healing in *Cana*—the centurion heard them in *Capernaum,* Matthew 8:5; John 4:46.
5. The nobleman's son had a *fever*—the centurion's servant a *paralysis,* Matthew 8:6; John 4:52.
6. The nobleman desired Christ to go home with him—the centurion deprecated His going, Matthew 8:7; John 4:49.
7. At Cana Christ speaks the word only, and does not go down to the house—at Capernaum He apparently did both, Matthew 8:13; Luke 7:7; John 4:49, 50.
8. At Cana, Jesus blames half-faith in the demanding of signs and wonders—at Capernaum He marvels at the fullness of faith, Matthew 8:10; John 4:48.

The centurion, whose title means that he was the commander of a hundred soldiers or more in the Roman army, was a Gentile, and Gentiles were generally despised by the Jews, but this Gentile suppliant who had all the marks of a Christian gentleman was respected by Jews and Gentiles alike. The Jews appreciated him because he had built a synagogue, at his own expense, for them, and begged Jesus to heal his servant. As for the Gentiles, those who served under him obeyed his orders, not only because they had to, but because they respected him as a man and as their commander. Ellicott says of him that he exhibited "a purity, reverence, simplicity, nobleness of life not found in any heathen religion. Loved alike, then, by Jew and Gentile, such a breakdown of the barrier, foreshadowed the spiritual brotherhood in Christ, in which there is neither Jew nor Gentile."

Accustomed to command, the centurion was capable of genuine concern for his sick servant. As the word for servant is *slave*, this needy one was not treated as a human chattle, but more like a son, for Luke says he was *dear* or precious to his master, a most unusual attitude of wealthy Romans towards their slaves. Thus, the centurion blended affection with authority, and knowing all about Jesus as a teacher endowed with supernatural power, brought the information to Him of his slave's pressing need of healing; and his earnest plea revealed that his heart was touched with pity over the suffering of his valued servant. Had it been his own son he could not have shown more care and concern.

That the centurion came to Jesus believing in His ability to heal is evident in his request, "Speak the word only, and my servant shall be healed" (Matthew 8:8). He did not ask for a sign, as Gideon did, for a manifestation of the ability of Jesus to heal, or urge Him to come to his home, pray over his servant, and touch him. C. H. Spurgeon says, "The centurion's staggering faith required no clutch." His was a grand faith, asking for no visible sign, but only the uttering of a word. As a man of authority, and under authority, he knew that personal presence was not necessary, for he could delegate his soldier or his slave to obey his orders. So, as he sent his friends to meet Jesus, he argued that because of His sovereignty, He could exercise His will through His words, and that would be sufficient, and, as we shall further indicate he received a gracious reward for his great faith.

What particularly impresses our minds about this anxious man's solicitation of the One he believed had the authority and power to bid diseases obey His will, was his modesty, reticence, and reverence in his approach to Jesus. While the elders of the Jews said to Jesus, "He was worthy for whom he should do this" (Luke 7:4), the centurion himself was possessed by the thought of his own unworthiness and said to Jesus, "I am not worthy that thou shouldest enter my roof: Wherefore neither thought I myself worthy to come unto thee" (Luke 7:6, 7). It was this innate modesty that brought the centurion to his finest hour, for he pressed his plea for healing with decorum and ease, and in such an approach revealed true reverence for Jesus, who alone is worthy. An ancient proverb reminds us that "Modesty cannot be taught, it may be born." The centurion's sincere reticence was inborn.

His was no false humility, neither was he proud of his humility as, alas! some are. The comment of Augustine is apt, "He counted himself unworthy that Christ should enter his doors, he was counted worthy that Christ should enter his heart." The Lord ever has respect toward the humble in heart. Ellicott's comment is, "The sense of unworthiness implied at once the consciousness of his own sins, and the recognition of the surpassing holiness and the majesty of the Teacher addressed."

Such modesty and confidence in the efficacy of Christ's Word to heal the dying servant without Him being in his sick chamber aroused Christ's commendation, and received a rich reward. As He made His way to the centurion's house, saying, "I will come and heal him" (Matthew 8:7), the boy was healed at that very hour. There had been no slow abatement of the slave's disease, but an immediate departure of it. "The healing word flowed from Jesus as naturally as the perfume from the flowers."

A saying, attributed to Horace, the ancient Roman poet reads, "Modesty, and Faith unstained, sister to Justice, and naked truth," are qualities that can be applied to the centurion for Christ, marveling at his unstained modesty and faith included both in His commendation, "I have not found so great faith, no, not in Israel" (Luke 7:9). His faith was indeed "great" in that, as a Gentile, he had no claim in his own right to the mercy and ministry of Jesus, but believing as he did he revealed that the principle of faith is supreme over all privileges of race and birth. This noble Roman soldier then, by his confidence in Jesus, reached *the finest hour* of his life and became the morning star of Western faith.

21

The Woman With an Issue of Blood and Her Fine Hour of Contact

ACTUALLY, in the context in which this miracle is found, we have a miracle within a miracle, as it happened when Jesus was on His way to heal the dying daughter of Jairus (Luke 8:40–56). Sandwiched in between the two halves of another miracle, we can call the healing of the woman a *parenthesis* miracle. On one errand of mercy, Jesus found another merciful work to accomplish as He went about doing good. This story vividly illustrates the constant ministry of Jesus while in Galilee. Meeting with the woman on His way to Jairus might have seemed an interruption, but what a blessed one it was for the afflicted woman! Alas! when we are extremely busy we resent any interruption, but Jesus knew how to turn an interruption to good account, namely, the relief of another needy heart.

Although the primitive church identifies this woman as Veronica, the woman who walked with Jesus to His cross, and seeing His blood and sweat, took her handkerchief and wiped His brow, and found the image of His bloodstained face imprinted upon the linen, she remains

113

one of the anonymous female characters in the Gospels. What compelled her to seek Jesus was the failure of medical men to relieve her of the malady she had suffered from for twelve years. The account of her story reads, she had "spent all her money upon physicians, neither could be healed of any. She grew worse." But as we are to see, where human physicians failed, the great Physician succeeded, for with Him all things are possible, as the swift healing of the woman's disease testifies. Although she came as a last resort to Jesus, she was rewarded.

Because of her hemorrhage lasting for twelve years she was rendered legally unclean, and, therefore, not qualified to present herself to Jesus and state her pressing need. So her uncleanness, coupled with her humility, and the pressure of the crowd made close contact with the Healer almost impossible. But believing in His power to cure her without payment, she succeeded in spite of the crowd thronging Jesus to touch Him. Many must have touched Him as they were so close to Jesus, but only one touched Him by faith, and in doing so came to her *finest hour*, for "straightway the fountain of her blood was dried up" (Mark 5:29).

How swift Jesus was in the relief of the suffering! He spoke, touched or willed, and it was done. His instantaneous power to save the soul is a miracle multitudes can also testify to. To quote from my work on *All the Women of the Bible*:

> The term Jesus used in addressing the nameless sufferer, *Daughter*, suggests she was still young, though wasted and faded by a malady which made her look older than she was. But the nature of her disease and the age of the afflicted one made no difference to Him in healing the sick and saving the lost. As Jesus passed by

the withered fingers of the woman brushed the border
of Christ's sacred dress, and all at once her thin body
felt the painless health of her childhood return. A
strength she had not known for twelve years renewed
her being, and she knew that Christ had made her
whole.

Another remarkable feature of this miracle is the fact
that as soon as the woman touched the dress of Jesus, He
perceived that healing power had gone out from Him.
Peter mildly rebuked Jesus for thinking that it was possible to identify anyone touching Him with such a crowd
pressing close upon Him. But as the omniscient Lord, He
knew within His own mind that some needy soul, believing that He could heal all manner of diseases, had touched
Him, hence His question, "Who touched me?" The touch
of faith could not be hidden from Him even though the
woman's touch was unnoticed by the rest of the crowd,
many of whom had also touched Him but with no result.
It added to the woman's finest hour when she immediately acknowledged receipt of the cure received. The
Physician quickly identified the patient who saw that
"she could not be hid" any longer, and humbly and grate-
fully, she fell at the feet of her Benefactor, and declared the
immediate healing she had received simply by a touch.
We can imagine what a glow and health of countenance
must have been hers as she publicly witnessed that her
burden for twelve years had vanished. The commendation of Jesus for her faith must also have contributed to
such a sublime hour. As a true daughter of Abraham, the
benediction of Jesus, must have consoled her heart, as He
used the endearing term "Daughter," as friendly be-
nignity she never forgot. "Be of good comfort: thy faith
hath made thee whole" (Matthew 9:22). As for ourselves

every hour is a fine hour when, as an unknown author reminds us,

> We touch Him in life's busy throng,
> And we are whole again.

The saving and healing power of Jesus can be experienced any hour when by faith we take hold of His skirt (Zechariah 8:23). What the woman received from Jesus was *freely* provided. As a sufferer, she had spent all her money seeking relief from physicians without avail; but what she sadly needed, Jesus performed as a gift. Thus, is it with ourselves. Whatever we come to Him for, in accordance with His will, we receive without money, and without price.

As the two halves of the contact of Jairus are like two arms enfolding the middle miracle of the healing of the woman with an issue of blood, it is but fitting at this point to briefly comment on the finest hour that came to this ruler of the synagogue. The context opens with a distressed father falling at Jesus' feet, pleading for the life of his dying twelve-year-old daughter—the same period the woman had endured her issue. Jesus immediately responded to the cry of Jairus for help and went with him to his home. But on the way, the miracle just considered happened. As one of the princes of the Jewish synagogue, Jairus knew about the remarkable teachings and miracles of Jesus, and so with his only daughter at death's door, he sought the Miracle Worker on her behalf.

After the miracle "on the wing," which must have strengthened his faith in the ability of Jesus to heal his daughter as He had the woman with an issue, Jesus continued His journey with Jairus to his shadowed home, but on the way a messenger from the ruler's house, met the company with the sad news, "Thy daughter is dead;

trouble not the Master" (Luke 8:49). But having met the Master, somehow the sting of such a dread announcement was not felt by the sorrowing, yet confident, father, who reached his finest hour—the fine hour of relief—when Jesus comforted his heart by saying, "Fear not, believe only, and she shall be made whole" (Luke 8:50). What a staff to lean upon that was in the shadow of death.

Reaching the house, Jesus found relatives and friends weeping and wailing over the dead girl, and they laughed Him to scorn when He said, "Weep not; she is not dead but sleepeth" (Luke 8:52). All curious and unbelieving onlookers were put out of the chamber, and only the girl's parents and Peter, James, and John witnessed the miracle Jesus performed in the atmosphere of faith. Standing by the little bed, Jesus took one of the girl's cold hands and tenderly said, "Maid, arise" (Luke 8:54), and immediately the dead girl revived, got out of bed and walked, and her parents who had come to *their finest hour* were astonished. The command to the dead was as brief as in the case of Lazarus—"Come forth!"

Then, a delightful thoughtfulness, Jesus told the parents to give the child something to eat. How kind and considerate Jesus was, even when it comes to details! Being able to eat again proved the reality of the miracle, and we can imagine what a tasty and satisfying meal those happy parents prepared. Then Jesus instructed them not to say anything about the miracle, as far as the outside world was concerned because He knew that it would be detrimental for the spiritual and bodily life of the precious girl to become the object of the visits of those bent on idle curiosity. As for Jesus Himself, His fame spread "abroad through all the land," as the Conqueror of death.

22

Peter and His Fine Hour of Intuition

WE READILY AGREE with the sentiment that Peter is one of the most compelling and fascinating characters in New Testament history, which is borne out by Alexander Whyte's paragraph in his *Bible Characters:*

> The Four Gospels are full of Peter. After the name of our Lord Himself, no name comes up so often as Peter's name. Our Lord speaks oftener to Peter than to any other of His disciples: sometimes in praise, sometimes to blame. No disciple speaks so often and so much as Peter. No disciple is so pointedly reproved by our Lord as Peter, and no disciple ever ventures to reprove his Master but Peter. No other disciple ever so boldly confessed and outspokenly acknowledged and encouraged our Lord as Peter repeatedly did, and no one ever intruded, and interfered and tempted Him as repeatedly as Peter did.

Intensely human, Peter had his faults for which he was repentant, but failures and triumphs were just stepping-stones by which this fisherman, who became an apostle, reached higher heights. This is why it is so exhilarating and encouraging to often study Peter's story if we would climb upward from our "dead selves to higher, better things." All the Gospels tell us about him is that his original name before he met Jesus was Simon; that he was a son of Jona, and a native of the small town of Bethsaida. When Andrew, his brother, brought him to Jesus, Peter received a strange salutation from Him, "Thou art Simon the son of Jona; thou shalt be called *Cephas* [*Kephas* as it should be pronounced], which is by interpretation, A stone" (John 1:42). At the time, this given name, meaning, a *rock*, appeared to be out of place for the fisherman had nothing of the steadfastness of a rock about him, but under the hand of the Master, Simon, which implies *listening* became Peter, a rock, a man of strong, firm character, whose strength came from the Rock of Ages Himself. So, the declaration *Thou art . . . Thou shalt be* was both a revelation and a prophecy, for Jesus saw latent possibilities under the surface of a rough exterior, and with prophetic insight of the mighty force he would become, gave him his new name of Peter. That the prophecy of Jesus was verified is proven by the apostle's rocklike character, the Acts presents.

As scores of study and devotional books have been written about Peter's life and labors and literature, it is impossible for us in four or five pages to describe all the stirring scenes in his history; and because in our meditations we have been seeking to select the finest hour in the lives of those presented, we must confine ourselves to such a conspicuous hour in the career of this great man of "brawn and action." We are cognizant of the fact that opinions may differ among Bible lovers, as to the most sublime hour Peter faced. Some may affirm that it took place when Andrew introduced him to Jesus, and the miracle happened and they became one forever. Truly, this was the foundational hour in Peter's life, and one he never forgot.

Others may decide that Peter came to his finest hour on the Mount of Transfiguration when he saw Jesus glorified, and had converse with Moses and Elijah who came down from heaven. That this marvelous hour left an indelible impression on Peter's heart is seen in his later reference to beholding the Lord's glory when he was with Him on the holy mount. Further, we can understand why others take Pentecost as Peter's finest hour, seeing it was a momentous hour resulting in a mighty, spiritual revival in which the apostle became the chief figurehead.

Our personal selection of Peter's finest hour, however, was the one he experienced when he witnessed to the true identity of Jesus, and gave to the church its first Christian creed. By this time, the Twelve had been with Jesus for more than a year, studying His life and teachings and feeling the impact of them in their own lives. His miracles, also, begat a strong faith in His omnipotence. Then, although Jesus knew all that His disciples felt about Him, one day He asked them, "Whom do men say that I the Son of man am?" They answered, "Some say that thou art John the Baptist: some Elias, and others, Jeremias, or one of the prophets" (Matthew 16:13, 14).

Then, looking into the eyes of Peter, Jesus asked the disciples, "But whom say ye that I am?" and immediately, by the Spirit's intuition, Peter answered, "Thou art the Christ, the Son of the living God" (Matthew 16:15, 16). Jesus had warned His own that a fanatic here and there would rise saying, "I am Christ," but Peter, sensing the messiahship and deity of the Man before him confessed, "Thou art *the* Christ." Peter reached the pinnacle of revelation when he saw in Jesus, One who dwarfed the spiritual leaders of the ages. And that this was his finest hour is attested to by the benediction of the One, Peter has confessed:

> Blessed art thou, Simon Bar-jona: for flesh and blood hath not revealed it unto thee, but my Father, which is in heaven.
>
> Matthew 16:17

Then came the astounding declaration of Jesus:

> I also say unto thee, That thou art Peter, and upon this rock I will build my church; and the gates of hell shall not prevail against it.
>
> Matthew 16:18

Here we have our Lord's first mention of a new society, *My church*, which was to be built,, not upon Peter,r, as some erroneously teach, but upon the One Peter confessed as "the Christ, the Son of the living God" (Matthew 17:16). This is the pillar and ground of truth of the church of the living God, and other foundation can no man lay (1 Corinthians 3:11; 1 Timothy 3:15). Christ alone is the foundation and chief cornerstone of the mystic fabric He called *My church*—a truth from *his finest hour*, Peter never lost sight of.

23

The Prodigal Son and His Fine Hour of Contrition

DR. GRIFFITH THOMAS SPEAKS of the renowned fifteenth chapter of Luke's Gospel as "a masterpiece of writing and an inspired revelation of the heart of God." Approaching a study of this *one* parable with its three pictures, we find ourselves embarrassed by spiritual riches, for in it we have the work of the Trinity in redemption so impressively portrayed. Frank W. Boreham, in his small work, *The Prodigal Son,* has a most interesting chapter on "The Trilogy of Jesus," in which he says that the three incomparable illustrations He used are not "isolated drawings but three panels of one panel." Unity of thought in Luke 15 is also stressed by C. H. Spurgeon:

> The three parables recorded in this chapter are not repetitions; they all declare the same main truth, but each reveals a different phase of it. The three parables are three sides of a pyramid of Gospel doctrine, but there is a different inscription upon each . . . . Each one of the parables is needful to the other, and when combined they present us with a far more complete

exposition of their doctrine than could have been conveyed by any one of them.

The Sheep was lost, and probably knew it had strayed from the fold and care of the shepherd, but happily he found it and carried it home. How full of the truth this first picture is of the love of Jesus, the Good Shepherd, who gave His life for the sheep! "I was lost, but Jesus found me."

The Coin was lost through the action of a person, and having no consciousness of being lost remained where it had dropped until it was recovered. If this particular piece of silver the woman lost was part of a woman's dowry which every married woman wore in a chain across her forehead, then in her we can discern the love of the Spirit for sinners, lost through no fault of their own, but still *lost*.

The Son was lost through his own deliberate action. His departure from home was self-determined, and proved him guilty of an inexcusable waywardness. But his father's heart went out to his younger son in spite of his folly and was overjoyed at his return. Here we have a graphic illustration of the Father-heart of God, as sinners turn to Him in true penitence and faith.

An ancient writer remarked that the key to this notable chapter is found hanging on the front door—"This man receiveth sinners, and eateth with them" (Luke 15:2). How one would delight in fully meditating upon the three stories teaching one truth—joined together by God—but such is not our aim, because of our effort to focus upon some particular episode in the life of those chosen, making it to represent their finest hour! It is for this reason that we concentrate upon the prodigal son in the parable

Jesus taught the self-righteous Pharisees, typified in the elder brother, in order to discover his most rewarding hour. While we call him a *prodigal,* and his heart-moving story has done more to win the prodigals and the down-and-outs of human society than any other part of the Bible, the Bible itself does not use the term prodigal.

Reading again this parable without equal in the literature, and which Charles Dickens described as "the finest short story ever written," one wonders why a son, tenderly cared for in a good home by a kind and loving father, should want to leave it. Perhaps, being young and free of marriage ties, he felt circumscribed and longed to stretch his wings, or see life in a far country he had heard about that offered everything for a young man's satisfaction. So the hour came, doubtless a glad hour to him, when he told his dear father of his decision and asked for the share of money laid aside for him, and left home.

This young son, with a desire for false independence, however, was soon to learn that a fool and his money are quickly and easily parted. In the paradise of pleasure he thought he had found, his father's bequest was soon squandered in wild living. With plenty of money to spend, he had plenty of friends, but with the vanishing of his money, there came the vanishing of his friends for in his dire need, no man was willing to give him even a bit to eat. Having yielded to his baser appetite, he was found in a piggery, feeding swine, and feeling as if he must appease his hunger by eating the food of swine, which was the beanlike pods of the carob tree.

But—and it is a blessed *but*—the wretchedness this prodigal was enduring stirred his reason into a resolution which was to be for him his finest hour. Deeply contrite because of his sensual and sexual desires, in the midst of his disillusionment and degradation, we read that "he came to himself." An ancient Jewish saying has it, "When Israel is reduced to the carob tree they become repentant." It was so with this young son far from home, and eager to return home. Our Lord used two suggestive phrases in this part of the story, namely, *He came to himself—He came to his father* (Luke 15:17, 20). Too many sinners come to themselves, and realize how lost and hell-deserving they are, but they fail to come to a heavenly Father, who waits to forgive them and take them home to His heart.

Perishing with hunger—a hunger intensified by the abundance of food in the old home he had forsaken, the prodigal reached his finest hour when he said:

> I will arise and go to my father, and will say unto him, Father, I have sinned against heaven, and before thee, And am no more worthy to be called thy son: make me as one of thy hired servants.
>
> Luke 15:18, 19

The development of this incomparably tender story is heartmoving. As the prodigal son arose to come to his father, the father was on his way to meet him. How did he know that his lost boy was returning home, when he had no way of sending word that he had resolved to return? Can it be that the loving father went out every day during his son's absence and scanned the horizon for a sight of him coming home? Often he had looked along the road by which the prodigal had traveled to the far country, and then one day it happened—"he saw when he was yet a great way off," and recognizing him by his height and gait, "had compassion, and ran, and fell on his neck and kissed him" (Luke 15:20).

Compassion here means that his heart beat quickly as he caught sight of his wandering boy. Then, what a delightful touch it is, *he ran*. The prodigal so weary, hungry, and remorseful could not run, but his aging father, forgetting his years and dignity, ran to meet his ragged and footsore boy. As for falling on his neck, and kissing him, what an unrestrained and overflowing manifestation of fatherly love this was. How suggestive all of this is of God's welcome for the penitent sinner, embracing him in His fatherly arms, and kissing the past into forgetfulness!

Still in his father's arms, the prodigal son commenced to recite the resolve he had framed, but his plea of contrition was never completed for his father never received that part of it, "Make me as one of thy hired servants" (Luke 15:19). That he was still worthy to be called his son, he said, "Bring forth the best [*first*] robe, and put it on him" (Luke 15:22), and his dirty, smelly rags were removed, as a token of his reinstating into full sonship, as also the *ring* and the *shoes* imply. The signet ring, symbol of the union of father and son, and shoes for his almost-naked feet signified his restoration into the household, whose members wore shoes, while the slaves were barefooted. Having received the full standing of a son there came the feasting and rejoicing over one who had been as good as dead, but was alive again; lost, but found. Such a fatherly welcome completed the prodigal's *finest hour*. How eloquent all this part of "the crown and pearl of all parables" is of the joy of a loving, forgiving God over a truly repentant sinner, and of the joy of a forgiven sinner in a "God of forgivenesses!" (*see* Daniel 9:9).

24

Two Asses and Their Fine Hour of Service

BECAUSE THE BIBLE gives us two instances of asses being divinely used, it will not be thought ludicrous to include them, stubborn though they be, in our roll of those humans who came to a finest hour. Creator of both man and beast, God is able to employ them to fulfill His purpose. If Satan could use a serpent to carry out his evil design, surely the Creator can employ His animal kingdom in any way He desires. That He has absolute dominion over beast and bird, is proven by many incidents in His Word. Here are some striking examples:

> The action of the raven and the dove to assure Noah of
> the flood's subsidence.
> The judgments upon Pharaoh—frogs, serpents, fish,
> lice, flies, cattle, and locusts.
> The provision of quails in the wilderness as food for a
> hungry multitude.
> The commanding of ravens to feed Elijah, the faithful
> yet famished prophet.
> The opening and shutting of the mouths of lions in

129

connection with Daniel's trial of faith.
The crowing of a cock to remind Peter of his shameful
denial of the Master.

All of these instances, and others, indicate the Creator's
supremacy in what we call the *dumb creation*, which in-
cludes Balaam's ass and our King's ass.

If the cattle on a thousand hills are the Lord's to do as
He wishes with so are asses. And how He delights to take
the weak and foolish things of this world to confound the
mighty! Modernists, who attempt to confine God to
natural law and, therefore, unable to intervene in the
natural course of events, reject the miracle of an ass speaking with a man's voice, and advance the explanation that
"by influencing the soul of Balaam, God caused him to
interpret correctly the inarticulate sounds of the animal."

Believing, however, that with God all things are possible we hold that in the record we have a literal narrative
setting forth a real transaction, and a combination of
miracles. The adequate cause of the ass speaking audibly,
and uttering words Balaam understood is given in the
phrase, "The Lord opened the mouth of the ass"—and
when God opens a mouth, an ass can speak as well as a
man who is sometimes described, because of his foolish-
ness, by the epithet of *an ass*. Without doubt, Balaam was
an ass of a man at the time because Peter reminds us that
"the dumb ass speaking with man's voice forbad the
madness of the prophet" (2 Peter 2:16). When Balaam became fully adjusted to the will of God, we read that He put
words in his mouth to utter to Balak (Numbers 23:16).

Balaam's ass reached its finest hour when it saw "the
angel of the Lord," a phrase used four times in the narrative. What a contrast—*angels* and *asses!* Yet the Lord

brought an angel and an ass together for the accomplishment of His purpose. As Andrew M. Fairbairn states it in
his erudite work on *Miracles:*

> The plain historical statement need give no trouble to
> those who believe that the serpent spoke with Eve:
> another might well do the same as an instrument of the
> great Angel of the Covenant . . . An ass was chosen, in
> the sovereignty of God, to rebuke the covetous eager-
> ness of Balaam for reward, human reason and speech
> being miraculously conferred on her for the occasion.

The ass saw the angel with "his sword drawn in his
hand" (Numbers 22:23), a symbol of the execution of divine justice. Thus, the beast saw what Balaam could not
see until "the Lord opened the eyes of Balaam, and he saw
the angel of the Lord standing in the way, and his sword
drawn in his hand; and he bowed down his head, and fell
flat on his face" (Numbers 22:31). As the ass saw that the
angel stood in the way, it turned aside to go into the field,
but Balaam forced it back into the road, then the angel
intervened and forced the animal against a wall, crushing
the prophet's foot against it. But as there was no way to
turn because of the angel's blockade, Balaam's temper
rose and he smote the poor but privileged creature, and
then another miracle took place, for it not only saw a
visitor from heaven, but spoke with the voice of a man.

It added to the ass's finest hour, when the Lord opened
its mouth, and rebuked the prophet for his threefold beat-
ing. Balaam replied that if he had had a sword with him
he would have killed the disobedient ass. Then came its
remarkable, divinely given plea, "Am not I thine ass,
upon which thou hast ridden ever since I was thine unto

this day? was I ever wont to do so unto thee? And he said, Nay" (Numbers 22:30). Thus God gave the creature both vision and vocal power. Whether it understood the presence of the militant-looking angel, or its own articulation, we do not know. What is clearly apparent is the contrast between the animal's instinctive obedience and the prophet's self-willed disobedience, which brought him to a humiliating hour so different to his ass's fine and famous hour.

But Balaam came to learn that God's miraculous use of his faithful ass was necessary to teach him that the same divine power causing the dumb creature to speak contrary to nature could enable the prophet himself to utter blessings contrary to his own inclination. So, as the Lord had opened the mouth of the ass, He also opened the mouth of Balaam, as He had previously opened his eyes, and he blessed those Balak had hired him to curse. The remarkable prophecies concerning Israel as found in Numbers 23 and 24, are the words that came out of the divinely controlled mouth of Balaam—great words that sprang out of a dumb ass that had one *finest hour* in its otherwise drab existence.

A French proverb has it, "An old ass is never good." Perhaps this is why Jesus chose a *colt,* the foal of an ass for His triumphant entry into Jerusalem. A German proverb reads that "An ass loaded with gold climbs to the top of the castle." This we know, that the ass, with Jesus as its load, climbed to the top of the animal creation in privilege as it carried its Creator, and in so doing reached its finest hour. G. K. Chesterton, in his verses on "The Donkey" uniquely describes the contempt of those who can see nothing laudable in such a creature, and think of it as only:

The devil's walking parody
On all four-footed things.

But the poet imagines the proud feeling of the ass, as it bore Jesus into the city, and came thereby to its fine hour, and exclaimed:

Fools! For I also had my hour;
One far fierce hour and sweet:
There was a shout about my ears,
And palms before my feet.

What transpired on that first Palm Sunday when "came Christ the swordless on an ass," as crowds of pilgrims following Him, wondering whether He would at last announce Himself as King and claim His kingdom, seeing "they thought the kingdom of God should immediately appear" (Luke 19:11), is full of spiritual instruction for our hearts. First of all, there was the request of Jesus that two of his disciples go to a nearby village, where they would find an ass with its colt, and to bring them to Him. If the owner of same demurred they were to say, "The Lord hath need of them, and straightway he will send them" (Matthew 21:3). Possibly the owner was also a disciple and knowing Jesus was a King obeyed without hesitation. Kings, in those days, never hired or asked permission for the right to use the animals of their subjects; they simply annexed them. Then, in turn, we have the following aspects of the colt episode.

A Prophecy Fulfilled. Hundreds of years before Jesus appeared, Zechariah was given the prophecy, "Rejoice greatly, O daughter of Zion; shout, O daughter of Jerusalem: behold, thy King cometh unto thee: he is just, and having salvation; lowly, and riding upon an ass, and upon a colt the foal of an ass" (Zechariah 9:9), and Jesus distinctly declared that His entry into Jerusalem was the fulfillment of the ancient prophecy. Whether the disciples fully understood at that time the significance of such a fulfilled prophecy, we do not know, but Jesus claimed His fulfillment of it in the way He rode into the city. Certainly, the disciples wanted their Master to claim His kingdom, but it was to be one on which they might sit on His right hand and on His left, and not in the kind of kingdom He spoke of as being "not of this world," or like its earthly kingdoms maintained by force. Jesus often laid hold of Old Testament prophecies and related them to Himself with the usual formula—"It is written of me." As for godly Jews, their long wistfulness for the coming of the promised Messiah enabled them to link Christ's appearance on the colt, without any hesitancy, with the forecast of Zechariah's prophecy.

A Royalty Displayed. The key phrase in the prophecy and in its fulfillment is, "Behold, thy King cometh unto thee" (Matthew 21:5)—but what an unrefined way to come, riding on the back of a young donkey! Kings and emperors, conquerors of earthly kingdoms, would ride in chariots with all the pageantry of royalty and victory. One cannot imagine a Roman emperor making a show of triumph on anything less than a magnificent steed. Yet, although the donkey was the conveyor of Jesus as He made His triumphant entry, He was nevertheless a true King, and rode as such. As the Prince of Peace, He chose the lowly pageantry of old referred to in the Song of Deborah, "Speak, ye that ride on white asses, ye that sit in judgment, and walk by the way" (Judges 5:10). Jesus had a rightful claim to kingship. He was *born* King of the Jews. Pilate asked Him, "Art thou a King then?" and He replied, "Thou sayest that I am a king. To this end was I born" (John 18:27). He will yet be seen as the King of kings. That the populace recognized His kingship is evident from the way they carpeted His way with branches of palm trees, and spread their garments over the road, the recognized homage paid to a king, and cried, "Hosanna in the highest" (Matthew 21:9). They had known Him as the prophet of Nazareth, now He rides as the King without a rival.

A Humility Illustrated. Although shouts of acclamation filled the air, esus rode silently and humbly, for the word "lowly" or "meek" used of Him means *humble.* There was no extravagance or arrogance about His entry for His victories were not won by the blood of His subjects. As Matthew Henry expresses it:

> There was nothing stately or magnificent about His retinue. He had His attendants—*a very great multitude*—the common people graced the solemnity of Christ's triumph, and none but such. Christ is honoured by the multitude, more than by magnificence, of his followers, for He values men by their souls, not by their preferments, names, or titles of honour.

He was not decked with gorgeous dress and decorations, but only with His rough homespun garment. Yet He rode in the best of dress, for He was clothed with humility, and manifested His humility in choosing an ass to ride on. Asses were made for service, not for state occasions—to carry burdens, not to be used in battles.

A Sovereignty Exhibited. A phrase that grips our hearts in the event before us is that which Jesus told His disciples to say to the owner of the ass and colt if there was any reluctance on his part to let them go. "Ye shall say, The Lord hath need of them, and straightway he will send them'' (Matthew 21:3). As the King, He claimed them for His service, and so sat on the colt on which man had never sat. As the King, He had the right to be the first to ride on the animal. Are you not impressed by the fact that He needed a young ass for His service, and revealed His matchless sovereignty in using it to the full? How He delighted in taking the lowest of His creatures to illustrate His teachings! This is also true in His dealings with men who although poor, disadvantaged, and handicapped in many ways are needed and used by Him.

We have no way of knowing whether the dumb young donkey had any given consciousness at the time that it was carrying a King, as it joined its bray to the cheers of the multitude. Whatever its reaction may have been it was certainly its finest hour and an honor that would never be repeated. Legend has it that the donkey still bears the evidence of what Chesterton calls, "one for fierce hour and sweet." Not long after that triumphant entry into Jerusalem, Jesus was crucified outside the city wall, and the dark stripe running down the back of an ass, crossed by another at the shoulder is, according to tradition, a cross that was communicated to the creature in *its finest hour* when Our Lord rode on the back of an ass in His lowly entrance into the city.

25

Stephen and His Fine Hour of Martyrdom

ONE OF THE MOST CONSPICUOUS results of the advent of the Holy Spirit, on the historic day of Pentecost, was the fusion of the disciples into the beginning of the mystic fabric Jesus had called *My church.* To the holy, praying, expectant company of about 120 gathered together in the upper chamber, after the effusion of the Spirit, there were added to the infant church around 3,000 souls, with the Lord adding to the church *daily* such as should be saved. Then through the signs and wonders wrought by the apostles, multitudes of both men and women were added to the Lord. As to the great company that came to believe, all were of one heart and of one soul, and shared all their possessions, as Barnabas illustrated when he sold his land and gave the money to the church.

Another outcome of Pentecost was the throwing into prominence a few disciples, such as Peter, James, and John, pillars of the church who were to give Paul the hand of fellowship as he too became a member of the church Jesus founded. At the outset Peter dominated the scene, and by his Spirit-empowered words and works raised the anger of priests, Sadducees, and Pharisees alike, whose ire produced the first persecution of the newly formed church. Among the first deacons, appointed by the Twelve, who achieved eminence was Stephen who, although not named as an apostle, became the most outstanding of those chosen for the daily ministrations of the church. Spirit-possessed, he overleaped the limitations of his task as a supervisor of benevolences to become a man of faith and power and of great wisdom, a performer of miracles, and a most powerful preacher.

The potent ministry of Stephen brought about the opposition of the leaders of the synagogue, and because of his remarkable defense before the council of Jews in which he summarized Old Testament teachings and related them to Christ, he was cited as a blasphemer, apprehended, and cast out of the city to be brutally stoned to death, thus becoming the first martyr of the Christian church. The word martyr originally meant, a *witness*, one who gives testimony, or a *spectator of anything*, but with the cruel death of Stephen the term marked the beginning of one who died for his fidelity to Christ and His Word. Three times over the word is used:

> The blood of thy martyr Stephen (Acts 22:20).
> Antipas was my faithful martyr (Revelation 2:13).
> The blood of saints—the blood of the martyrs of Jesus
> (Revelation 17:6).

When Stephen was brought before the council, whose members were not able to resist his Spirit-inspired wisdom, he gave utterance to his remarkable speech. Fixing their eyes on him they were amazed as they saw his face change and become as the face of an angel (Acts 6:15). His countenance was illumined as by the radiance of a divine brightness. But such a face with the glow of an ardent zeal and the serenity of a higher wisdom—indicating a fine hour for Stephen—was soon to be battered by stones and bloodied.

As Stephen closed his witness before the Jewish leaders, he called them "betrayers and murderers" (Acts 7:52), because of the sentence of death they urged upon Pilate to pronounce upon Jesus. Such a true condemnation raised their brute passion, and resulted in a manifestation of animal ferocity as they stoned Stephen when he was on his knees praying. But this rage on the part of his enemies brought Stephen to his finest hour. If stones and clouts make martyrs, then the deathly stones about to be hurled at him made him the recipient of a most glorious vision, for Spirit-filled as he was, he "looked up stedfastly into heaven, and saw the glory of God, and Jesus standing on the right hand of God" (Acts 7:55). Could any sublime hour eclipse this one?

Stephen began his speech speaking of "the God of glory" (Acts 7:2), now his soul is bathed in that glory. As to the double mention of seeing Jesus *standing* on the right hand of God, such a posture has a double significance. Stephen had been courageously standing up for the defense of Jesus before those who rejected Him, now Jesus is standing up in approbation of His servant's noble and faithful witness, and also as a token that He will sustain through the severe trial before him. The further application of the *standing* pose of Jesus is that from *sitting* at the right of God, He had risen and was ready to welcome His follower, faithful unto death, as he entered the door of heaven. What a wonderful reception that must have been, after the Lord received his spirit.

Stones certainly broke the bones of Stephen, and produced his brutal form of death, but they could not destroy his desire to pray, and to pray for his murderers, for as he kneeled down, he cried with a *loud* voice, "Lord, lay not this sin to their charge" (Acts 7:60). As he thus prayed, he doubtless had the prayer of Jesus in mind, when being crucified between two thieves, "Father, forgive them, for they know not what they do" (Luke 23:34). Such a heartfelt prayer from the blood-bespattered lips of Stephen for forgiveness completed *his finest hour,* and ended in him falling *asleep,* a descriptive term of death. But only the body sleeps in death, never the soul of man.

That Stephen's martyrdom was his finest but terrible hour, is borne out by the fact that it resulted in the conversion of one who was to become the most notable stalwart of the faith in the early Church. A young man of about twenty-eight years of age, he consented to the death of Stephen, and as his part in the accusation and death of Stephen, stood while others laid their outer garments at his feet. This young man was the renowned Jew, Saul of Tarsus. His remarkable surrender to the One Stephen died for came about through the prayer and cruel death of the martyr, as he, when he became Paul the Apostle, testified to (Acts 22:20). What a striking conformation this transformation was of the saying of Tertullian that "The blood of martyrs is the seed of the Church"!

26

Paul and His Fine Hour of Obedience

As COUNTLESS VOLUMES have been written on the life and labors of this *Apostle Extraordinary*, as Dr. R. E. D. White named his remarkable work on every aspect of Paul's career, it is impossible to give a full portrait of this saintly adventurer for Christ in three or four pages. The reader may find much helpful material on this magnificent personality in the twenty-three page section devoted to him in my volume, *All the Apostles of the Bible*. By way of introduction to our general purpose to light upon the finest hour in the experience of those considered, however, we can take a passing look at the one, more fully described in the New Testament than any other personality—Our Lord excepted.

Dr. White, in his volume we have just mentioned, says that the purpose of his portrait of Paul, most renowned of all the apostles, was to make him live again for ordinary disciples of the twentieth century as:

> *The Greatest of Christians,*
> *Profoundest of Teachers,*
> *Staunchest of Friends,*

> *Most Intrepid of Adventurers,*
> *Most Dauntless of Sufferers,*
> *Most Winsome of Saints,*
> *Paul of Tarsus, Soldier and Slave and*
> *Lover of Jesus Christ our Lord.*

From scattered references in the Acts, and also in Paul's own Epistles, one can arrive at an estimation of the background of this great biblical character, and outstanding in all history. Epochs in his career are as follows:

He was born in Tarsus of Roman parents—a fact significant in Paul's labors among Romans, as a free citizen of Rome.

He was the son of a Pharisee Jew and a Pharisee himself both by *birth* and *belief* regarding resurrection.

He had a strict religious training—was circumcised—knew Scripture—was familiar with Jewish history.

He was a tentmaker by trade, in keeping with Talmudic law instructing fathers to teach their sons the law and a trade.

His education was of the highest nature, with instruction from Gamaliel, the great philosopher, giving him knowledge of Greek poetry, philosophy, and literature.

His given name was Saul, meaning *asked for*, perhaps implying that he came as the son his parents asked God for. After his conversion he chose the name of Paul, signifying *small* or *little*, which had a connection with his small stature, probably less than five feet tall. According to tradition he changed his name in honor of Sergius Paulus, whom he led to Christ.

He was a persecutor of Christ and of His followers. An

ardent Pharisee, he was bent on stamping out the Christian faith. Although he consented to Stephen's death, there is no evidence that he himself had killed anyone.

He had a remarkable conversion, while making great havoc in the church, and never tired of speaking of his new life in Christ Jesus.

He became an outstanding missionary and church builder, in his travels in many directions.

He was a powerful preacher of the Word, and his sermons serve as models for preachers today.

He developed into a most gifted writer, authoring thirteen or fourteen of the New Testament twenty-seven books.

He died triumphantly for the Lord he dearly loved and served most faithfully.

From such a brief summary of a life which has been described as one of the greatest adventure stories of all time, we confine ourselves to the hour on that Damascus road, when God called him out of darkness and into His marvelous light. Suddenly, this saint hater, on his errand of threatening and slaughter, was arrested in a miraculous way—he had a revelation of the crucified Jesus as the living Christ, and thus became a witness of His resurrection—a qualification for apostleship. When he watched the angel face of Stephen, that became bloodstained through stoning, and then heard the martyr say, "I see the heavens opened, and the Son of Man standing at the right hand of God" (Acts 7:56), he thought that blasphemy, but now he sees Jesus for himself, and hears His voice asking why he persecutes *Him* in his cruel treatment of the saints.

Then Paul reached the finest hour of his life for recognizing Jesus, he asked, "Lord, what wilt thou have me to do?" (Acts 9:6). Then he received his marching orders to become a missionary to the Gentiles in order to turn them from darkness to light, and from the power of Satan to God. In reciting his divine transformation before King Agrippa, Paul said that he "was not disobedient unto the heavenly vision" (Acts 26:19). What finer hour could any man have than that of immediate and willing obedience to a command from heaven? Kipling has the phrase, "Be swift in all obedience," and Paul was certainly swift in his, which brought him to his most sublime hour. When he asked what the Lord would have him do, he was offering himself unreservedly to Him, and he never went back on that offer. Paul came to write, "his servants ye are to whom ye obey" (Romans 6:16), and *his finest hour* covered his marvelous ministry for he never faltered, even when in chains he called himself, "the prisoner of the Lord" (Ephesians 4:1), in obeying Him. Like His Master, Paul too, "became obedient unto death" (Philippians 2:8). Can we confess that we share the apostle's fine hour of obedience?

27

John and His Fine Hour in Patmos

THE WORLD OWES MORE than it will ever realize to literature that came out of prisons. Godly men and women find themselves incarcerated, often bound with chains, because of conscience sake, but those who held them in captivity could not bind their mind and spirit and pen. And so, by the grace of God they became fruitful in the land of their prison affliction, through the written works that came from such to enrich the lives of multitudes. "The mouth which persecution closes God opens, and bids it speak to the world," comments Ellicott. "If speech be silvern and silence golden, it is also true in the history of the Church that from the captivity of her teachers she has received her most abiding treasures." A few examples of this fact can be noted.

For his courageous witness for the great truths of the Gospel, the one-time monk, Martin Luther, found himself in Wartburg castle, but confinement could not curtail his mental activity, and so out of it came his unique translation of the Bible.

Another doughty warrior for Christ was the tinker of

145

Bedford, John Bunyan, whose cell in the Bedford jail was too feeble to silence the voice of God through him, and so out of it came his unique allegory and immortal classic, *Pilgrim's Progress* which, next to the Bible, has had the largest circulation of any book in the world.

Madame Jeanne Marie Guyon was another saint whose prison experiences only inspired her mind and pen to write some of the most impressive Christian poems. In one of these this renowned witness for the truth describes how she found a writing table in her barren wilderness.

> *A little bird I am,*
> *Shut from the fields of air;*
> *And in my cage I sit and sing*
> *To Him Who placed me there;*
> *Well pleased a prisoner to be,*
> *Because, my God, it pleases Thee.*
>
> *My cage confines me round;*
> *Abroad I cannot fly;*
> *But though my wing is closely bound,*
> *My heart's at liberty;*
> *My prison walls cannot control*
> *The flight, the freedom of the soul.*

Another stalwart defender of the faith whose prison walls could not control the freedom of his soul, was Samuel Rutherford, the seraphic soul who found himself being tried for treason. Deprived of his professorship in Saint Andrew's, this eminent Scottish covenanter found himself in the "bottle dungeon," as the city prison was named. But out of such a narrow cell with no door, but built like a bottle, prisoners were let down, or hauled up from the top, came Rutherford's fragrant *Letters*, so full of the glory and grace of the Master he dearly loved, and whom he called, "the ever-running over Lord Jesus."

For prison literature *par excellence*, however, we must turn to Scripture. It was while he was among the captives by the river of Chebar that the Prophet Ezekiel, by the Spirit, gave birth to his wonderful prophetic themes which were designed to keep before his fellow Jewish captives the national sins which had brought Israel so low. The captives felt they were best instructed by one who was a captive himself, and experimentally knew their sorrows.

Then we have the record of Paul, who was often in prison, and effectively used the experiences to further his mighty influence by his gifted pen—and for the extension of Christ's kingdom by the conversion of his fellow prisoners. Among his priceless writings to come out of confinement are Ephesians, Philippians, Colossians, and Philemon, known as the Prison Epistles.

We now come to John, who was banished to Patmos by the Emperor Nero, for "the word of God, and for the testimony of Jesus Christ" (Revelation 1:19). He had shared prison experiences before with Peter when both were apprehended for Christ's sake (Acts 4:3). But although his wings were somewhat bound, his heart was at liberty, and able to give the church one of the most dramatic books on the advent and victory of Christ ever written. When the church at Ephesus, which John had pastored, no longer heard him proclaiming the Word of God, his voice reached his late flock from his exile—as did other churches at that time, and the church of all time—through his highly symbolical book with its prominent, characteristic features of the struggle between good and evil and of all that will transpire when Christ appears.

There are two phrases in John's introduction to the Apocalypse compelling attention because of their combination; namely, *I was in the isle called Patmos—I was in the Spirit on the Lord's day.* Imprisonment in Patmos, where, perhaps, the apostle was free to roam within the boundary of the isle, did not interfere with his fellowship with the Christ above, whom he dearly loved. In fact, very little of the scenery of Patmos colors the Revelation. By the power of God, John was able to detach himself from the influence of outward surroundings—which brings us to *his finest hour.*

John was not only *in the isle*, but *in the Spirit.* Many are in the isle but never find their way into the Spirit. They never discover that prison walls cannot control the freedom of the soul. But for John on that memorable "Lord's Day," we call *Sunday*, the mind and spirit were drawn upward from things temporal to things spiritual—a spiritual abstraction the Holy Spirit alone can make possible, and ever does on the Lord's Day for saints who gather to hear yet once again, "I am Alpha and Omega, the first and the last" (Revelation 1:11).

The apostle had had many a fine hour before his Patmos imprisonment. What blessed hours this personification of love had spent with Jesus when He was in the flesh! Five times over he is described as "the disciple Jesus loved," and as the one who "leaned on Jesus' bosom." We can imagine what rapturous hours they had together. If, as old George Herbert expressed, "If David had his Jonathan, Christ had His John." Was it not this bond between them that enabled John, by the Spirit, to record in a book so many remarkable past, present, and prospective features of the One he dearly loved?

A noticeable feature about John as a writer is that although he withheld his name from the Gospel and three Epistles he wrote, he used it five times over in the last book of the Bible, the voice from heaven told him to write. What he was told to set forth was not Revelations, as his apocalyptic work is sometimes erroneously named, but the Revelation of Jesus Christ, that is the one, uninterrupted record of what he saw when he came to *the finest hour* of his life on that Lord's Day in his Patmos isle. It was because of this sublime hour that John gave us a book, of which Sir Isaac Newton said, "No other book can equal it in the dignity and sublimity of its composition."

In life, we, too, may find ourselves *in the isle*, or in a severely circumscribed environment, as a bird in a cage, as Madame Guyon puts it. If we resent our confinement, chafe under it, sigh to be delivered from it, it will only imprison us still more. But if we have learned to be *in the Spirit*, while *in the isle* of our Patmos, not only on the Lord's Day, but every day, then ours will be many a fine and blessed hour as we see Him, who is ever with His own in tribulation, and has "the keys of hell and of death" (Revelation 1:18), and can shut and open as He deems best.

28

Jesus and His Fine Hour of Completion

IN HIS HISTORICAL NOVEL, *The Heart of Midlothian*, Sir Walter Scott has the phrase, "The hour is come, but not the man." But in the most momentous hour in world history, the Man Christ Jesus was there, and made it a sacrificial hour, resulting in a glorious emancipation for a lost world from the guilt and government of sin. It was with some trepidation that we decided to include and conclude this particular line of meditation in the book before you with a short chapter dealing with the finest hour in the life of Jesus, because of the many surpassing exalted hours He experienced. He once said to His mother, "Mine hour is not yet come" (John 2:4), and latterly He could have confessed, "I have had many fine hours."

When He was only twelve years of age, Jesus had many a fine hour during His three days in the temple, hearing and answering questions, and astonishing the learned men sitting around Him with His unique wisdom and understanding. Then came the hour when His anxious parents retraced their footsteps and found Jesus in the temple, and rebuked Him for lagging behind. But His remarkable reply was a prophecy of the whole tenor of His life onwards, "Wist ye not that I must be about my Father's business?" (Luke 2:49).

Another inspiring and memorable fine hour was when He was baptized of John in Jordan and heard, as He emerged from the water, the voice of His Father, saying, "This is my beloved Son, in whom I am well pleased" (Matthew 3:17). With this benediction there was His baptism with the Spirit of God for service ahead.

As for His temptation in the wilderness, what a firm and fine hour of resistance was His, as He met every onslaught of the devil with the Word of God, and so defeated him that he left the Victor for a season.

The beginning of His public ministry, the call of His first disciples, and the performance of His first miracle must have thrilled the heart of Jesus. In fact, He had a fine hour in every miracle of His, and in every parable He taught, and in all His dealings with the sick and the sinful.

Then the Mount of Transfiguration was an awesome and glorious hour for Jesus, as His face shone as the sun and his raiment became white as light. Surely this must have been one of the finest hours for Peter, James, and John who were with Him, and beheld His glory. We leave the reader to trace other conspicuous hours in the work and witness of Him whose whole time was dedicated to the task assigned Him by His Father.

What arrests our minds, as we follow His steps through the Gospels, is His repeated reference to an hour, above all other hours, which was to come with all its gloomy yet glorious outcome—an hour, like some solitary mountain silhouetted against the horizon. We have the record of John as to the restraint of Christ's foes, as He witnessed against them in the treasury, "No man laid hands on him; for his hour was not yet come" (John 8:20). But that hour did come after the heartless betrayal of Jesus, when men laid hold of Him and prepared Him for the cross.

Then we have His anticipatory saying in His reply to the disciples' presentation of the request of the Greeks to see Jesus. "The hour is come, that the Son of man should be glorified" (John 12:23). He then went on to use the illustration of a harvest appearing from wheat that fell in the ground and died, and the connection between "the hour is come," and life from death. This was an hour, dark and dreadful, He did not want His Father to save Him from, since He was born to die in such a way. For Him, such an hour of travail was to be an hour of triumph, an hour when endless life would spring up from death. It was the truth George Matheson, the blind preacher and poet, expressed in poetic form as an hour for us to emulate, in his moving hymn, "O Love, That Will Not Let Me Go":

> *O Cross, that liftest up my head,*
> *I dare not ask to fly from Thee;*
> *I lay in dust life's glory dead,*
> *And from the ground there blossoms red*
> *Life that shall endless be.*

In His intercessory prayer, with eyes lifted up to heaven, Jesus prayed, "Father, the hour is come" (John 17:1), the hour of the dark path of death which He must tread before His return to the glory He had with the Father in His preexistent state before the world began. The cross was to finish the Saviour's Messianic mission, having glorified His mission on earth by dying as the sinless Substitute for sinners. The phrase, then, "I have finished the work thou gavest me to do" (John 17:4), cannot be confined to His unique ministry of some three years or so, simply because the crown and climax of the work God entrusted His beloved Son to accomplish was the death of the cross. Jesus viewed Calvary as being already endured and prayed, "Now I am no more in the world" (John 17:11), but He was still in the world and in the flesh, when He uttered these words. The immediate future of resurrection and ascension, after His death, was regarded as present. "I come to thee" (John 17:11).

With all these forward-looking utterances in mind we now come to His last and loud cry from the cross, "It is finished" (John 19:30), or, as the original expresses it in one triumphant word—*FINISHED!*—a word with the ring of victory in it for all to hear. Knowing that all things prophesied of Him were now accomplished, He gave vent to this exclamation of a perfect consummation. But what was finished? Not only the malice and enmity of His persecutors, humanly responsible for His death; not only His shame, sorrow, and suffering; not only the burdens bowing His head—His tears, bloody sweat, agony of body, and anguish of soul—but also a fulfillment of all things prophesied of Him in Scripture (John 19).

Types, promises, prophecies, and sacrifices—all foregleams of what Christ was to accomplish by His death—were abolished as He cried in triumph, *Finished!* His dying eyes saw those divine symbols He knew He would fulfill by His dying body. As He soared over the Alps of Agony, He reviewed the whole of the inspirited role of prediction and by His death procured the perfect consummation of them all. Not a single jewel of promise was left unfulfilled. It is somewhat significant that both Matthew and Mark, in their record of the Crucifixion, link the final hour of the death of Jesus with the rending of the temple curtain. "Jesus cried with a loud voice, and gave up the ghost. And the veil of the temple was rent in twain from the top to the bottom" (Mark 15:37, 38; Matthew 27:50, 51).

The method of sundering that beautiful massive curtain must not be overlooked. It was not rent from the bottom to the top by human hands, but from *top to bottom*, or from the heavenward end by God's own hand to the bottom, or earthward end; and by His rending of the veil, He sought to teach us many essential, glorious truths. Chief among these is the blessed fact that the way into the holiest of all is open to all through the rending of the Saviour's flesh as He died at Calvary.

That curtain had hitherto separated the holy place, from the Holy of Holies, into which section the high priest alone could enter, and he only once a year. To all others it was a closed and forbidden shrine. Of old, the saints would stand in awe wondering what lay behind that veil. But now there is no veil, and ours is the joyous confidence to enter God's secret place, and commune directly with Him without the intercession of any human priest. The glorious evangel of that sundered veil is that of the priesthood of all believers who have immediate access to God. Shadows were no longer necessary now that the Substance had come by that temple event, when all ceremonial law was abolished. Now, any sinner can "enter the holiest by the blood of Jesus, by a new and living way, which he hath consecrated for us through the veil, that is to say, his flesh" (Hebrews 10:19, 20. *See* 9:24, 25).

The phrase, "the veil of His flesh," merits attention. Jesus, in His human form, was the true Veil shrouding the Divine Glory from the eyes of men; but on the cross the

Veil was rent, and the glorious purpose of God in the salvation of a lost world was revealed. Alexander Smellie, in his heart-stirring devotional work, *In the Secret Place*, published over seventy years ago, has this inspiring paragraph on the unspeakable value of the death of Christ:

> If the beautiful curtain itself portrays the flesh of my Saviour, His divine-human person, His untainted character, His matchless life, what can the tearing of the curtain in two portray but His crucifixion, the decease which He accomplished at Jerusalem, His broken body, His blood poured forth? And this is the one way to God's heart and God's home—that Jesus, statelier, costlier, more resplendent than that which was the glory of the Jewish temple must die. I see Him paying the penalty on His Cross; making an end of my innumerable sins, so that, although they are sought for, they will never be found; working out my everlasting deliverance. I see Him, I trust Him, and I have redemption according to the riches of His grace. Through Him as the rent Veil I come to the reconciled God.

A further feature of the Gospel of Golgotha is that of God's purpose in the Incarnation being the Crucifixion. A virgin bore a Son, who was born for the express mission of becoming the Saviour of the world, who put the last stroke upon His coming by dying, and therefore claimed to be absolved from paying any further debt—*Finished!* Divine justice had been fully displayed, and now God was well-pleased to receive sinners to His heart; and Jesus, rejected by men, was now crowned with majesty and honor as the Redeemer. If His crucifiers failed to see it in the naked figure on the middle cross because of the unkingliness of the nail-pierced body, the thief who cried, "Lord, remember me" saw in Him One who was King indeed, One who would survive the horrible death of crucifixion, and establish another Throne, higher, nobler, and most lasting than any throne of the Caesars. "Lord, remember me when thou comest into thy kingdom" (Luke 23:42)—and the King did remember him in a bountiful way!

A veil of thick darkness covered Him from the sight of men, and in His travail, it seemed as if His Father's face was hid from Him, but at last He emerged a mighty Victor o'er His foes. Gates of brass were broken in pieces, and bars of iron cut asunder in that final, fatal yet finest hour when He cried aloud for heaven, hell, and earth to hear—*Finished!* In such a perfect consummation to His coming in the likeness of those He died to save, Jesus saw of the travail of his soul, and was satisfied. In the past counsels of Eternity, the Triune God conceived the plan of Redemption, and so He came, as the Lamb slain *before* the foundation of the world; and He now delights in us, not because He redeemed us, but because He redeemed us seeing He delighted in us in the dateless past. Before the world began, and man appeared as the Eternal One, He was able to look down the vista of ages to come and love a world not yet created.

Let us hear it anew from the Saviour's life, that He died to end transgression, and deal a fatal blow to Satan and sin, death and hell. He looked down with bloodshot eyes upon a devil-driven world and upward to heaven and cried—*Finished!* Sin shall have no further dominion over you. As C. H. Spurgeon once expressed it:

The champion entered the lists to do battle for our soul's redemption, against all our foes. He met sin, Horrible, terrible, all-but omnipotent Sin nailed Him to the cross; but in that deed, Christ nailed Sin also to the tree. There they both did hang together—Sin, and Sin's destroyer. Sin destroyed Christ, and by that destruction Christ destroyed Sin.

> *My sin—O the bliss of this glorious tho't—*
> *My sin—not in part, but the whole,*
> *Is nailed to the cross and I bear it no more:*
> *Praise the Lord, praise the Lord, O my soul!*
>   H. G. SPAFFORD

Blood, sweat, and tears, Jesus had all these in abundance, and when all blood-bespattered He entered the dark arena He laid hold of principalities and powers, and wickedness in high places, stripped them of the dominion over men, and rolling back all hellish forces, took the prey from the mighty, and dying, cried triumphantly— *Finished!* As long as the world lasts, there will never be another hour comparable to that finest hour of the Lamb of God when He bore away the sin of the world. What a grim yet glorious hour that was for Him as He came from Bozrah with garments crimson dyed!

True, He died in combat with sin, hell and the devil, but in dying, He slew death which failed to keep its prey: and the five bleeding wounds He bore, and still bears are the insignia of His perfect and permanent victory over Satan, and over the gloomy caverns and depths of hell. Thus, His life was not taken, but freely given for man's redemption. The action of His death was voluntary, for He had the power to lay down His life, and take it up again which He did in His resurrection. After uttering His final word of conquest He dismissed His spirit. Bowing His head, as if composing Himself to sleep, after accomplishing His God-given task, He died.

> There lies beneath its shadow,
>   But on the farther side,
> The darkness of an awful grave
>   That gapes both deep and wide;
> And there between us stands the Cross,
>   Two arms outstretch'd to save,
> Like a watchman set to guard the way
>   From that eternal grave.
>
> ELIZABETH C. CLEPHANE

We began our meditations by thinking of God's Fine Hour of Approbation, when after creating the heavens and the earth, and all that in them is, He saw that everything He had created was good—*very good*. We finish our coverage of those who reached a fine hour in life, with God's beloved Son, who surveying all that His death accomplished in bringing about a new creation, could also say, with His Father, *very good*—FINISHED! If the world should last for a thousand more years, multitudes of redeemed souls will still say, as they look up in love and reverence to the smitten Lamb, seated on His throne:

Lord Jesus, Calvary was Thy finest hour!

A Final Word. If, as Samuel Johnson has reminded us to "Learn that the present hour alone is man's," then our solemn obligation, as those who are the recipients of Christ's finished work, is to give each passing hour something to keep in store for eternity—to live each hour in the orbit of His will, thereby making all our hours fine and fruitful.